Biblical Basics

for

Believers

by Matt Costella

Fundamental Evangelistic Association
Los Osos, California

Biblical Basics for Believers

Copyright © February 2002
Fundamental Evangelistic Association

All rights reserved. No part of this book may be reproduced in any form, except for the inclusion of brief quotations in a review or article, without written permission from the author or publisher.

All Scripture quotations are taken from the
King James Version of the Bible.

To order additional copies of this book or to inquire about
pricing information or bulk quantities, please contact:

Fundamental Evangelistic Association
P. O. Box 6278
Los Osos, CA 93412
(805) 528-3534 (phone)
(805) 528-4971 (fax)

Library of Congress Control Number: 2002090554
ISBN: 0-9718516-0-3

Printed in the USA by

MORRIS PUBLISHING
3212 East Highway 30 • Kearney, NE 68847 • 1-800-650-7888

Contents

Preface

Almost 2000 years ago, the Holy Spirit led the apostle Peter to challenge men and women of God to be people who are continuously "grow[ing] in grace, and in the knowledge of our Lord and Saviour Jesus Christ" (2 Pet. 3:18). How well have we heeded this much needed exhortation? How well have we taken the time and exerted the effort to either grow in the knowledge of Jesus Christ ourselves or to help another brother or sister in Christ grow spiritually? It is clearly evident that the only way in which we can know about our Savior and His will for our lives is through the study of the pages of His Word to us, the Bible. Therefore, we "grow in knowledge" and we grow closer to Him through the diligent, consistent study of the holy Scriptures.

Today, the church is being bombarded with books, programs and seminars designed to meet the perceived needs of the Christian community. But these books, programs and seminars are doing little to immerse the believer in that which he truly needs: an accurate understanding of God's will for his life as revealed through the teaching of God's inerrant Word. What we believe will determine how we act, how we live, how we think and how we relate and respond to others as well as to our Lord Himself. Therefore, doctrine, the pure teaching of the Word of God, is extremely important. *Biblical Basics for Believers* is specifically designed to direct the new Christian as well as the growing Christian into a program of discipleship through a careful study of the teaching (doctrine) of the Word of God and the application of Biblical doctrine to everyday living.

Biblical Basics for Believers is by no means an exhaustive treatment of Biblical doctrine. Rather, it is a place to start, a guide that directs the reader into God's Word so he might better understand the basic truths of the Christian faith and the process of living the Christian life. May all who study the contents of this book in conjunction with the Word of God walk away from their time with God full of praise and glory to Him, not only for His great salvation, but for giving His children the strength and ability to know Him better and to serve Him in sincerity and truth.

How to Use This Book

Biblical Basics for Believers is intentionally designed to be flexible enough for use by believers of all ages in a variety of settings:

- ✔ Personal study
- ✔ One-on-one discipleship training
- ✔ Group study
- ✔ Sunday school or youth group classes

It has been written in an organized, easy-to-follow outline format which makes it especially "user friendly" in a classroom or group-study setting. However, regardless of whether or not this book is being studied by one or many, **Biblical Basics for Believers must be read and studied in conjunction with an open Bible.** To open *Biblical Basics for Believers* and read through it as one would read any other book will not enable the reader to gain the necessary insight and instruction from the Word of God that every believer should strive to obtain. *Biblical Basics for Believers* is merely a tool. The Word of God alone is the living, powerful source that, in concert with the Holy Spirit of God, changes lives, teaches Truth and convicts men, women and children of their sin and need for repentance. Therefore, each time a Scripture reference is mentioned, be sure to look up the reference and read it carefully.

Likewise, never begin a study of the Word of God without first praying to God and asking Him to reveal to you truths from His Word that He would have you to know and understand. It is the prayer of the writer that *Biblical Basics for Believers* will guide you into a closer relationship with God through topical, systematic and expository teaching of God's holy Word.

1

Salvation

Being a Christian means having a relationship—a relationship with the Creator of the heavens and the earth, a relationship with the One who loves us so much that He died for us though we did not deserve it nor even desire it. The most important decision any individual will ever make is the decision to receive God's gift of eternal life through faith alone in the person and work of Jesus Christ or to reject this precious gift. Those who accept it will become new people. Those who reject it will continue to be "dead in trespasses and sins" (Eph. 2:1). Salvation is necessary due to our sin, it is possible through Christ's death and resurrection, it is attainable through faith alone in the person and work of Jesus Christ and it is infinitely beneficial to all who receive it.

I. Salvation Is Necessary Due to Sin

A. Sin can be defined as anything contrary to the character of God. God is holy, righteous, just and separate from any evil or wickedness. Conversely, all humans are sinners by their very nature at birth as well as by the deeds they commit. In the eyes of God, all men are created equally guilty, for all men are descendents of Adam, the first sinner. Romans 5:12 says, "Wherefore, as by one man sin entered into the world, and death by sin; and so death passed upon

1

all men, for that all have sinned." No one is exempt, for God's Word declares that "all have sinned and come short of the glory of God" (Rom. 3:23). Both physical and spiritual death are the results of sin, for God's Word declares that "the wages of sin is death" (Rom. 6:23). Because every individual is born as the offspring of a sinner, Adam, we are all tainted with the evil and wickedness that are an offense to the very nature of God. All who die in this sinful state will suffer eternal damnation in the lake of fire, for "it is appointed unto men once to die, but after this the judgment" (Heb. 9:27). God's Word says, "Whosoever was not found written in the book of life was cast into the lake of fire" (Rev. 20:15).

B. The Bible describes unregenerate sinners as "enemies" of God who live under His wrath. In Ephesians 2:3, Paul writes that we "were by nature the children of wrath." To the church at Rome, he described the unsaved as "ungodly," "sinners" and "enemies" of God (Rom. 5:6-10). It is evident from Scripture that sin is not only a lack of righteousness or conformity to God's character and will, but it is actual opposition to the divine will of God (Rom. 5:10; 8:7).

C. Every aspect of our being is tainted by sin—our mind or intellect, our emotions, our will and our physical bodies. Every individual is born into this world as a sinner and, therefore, is totally incapable on his own of reaching God or obtaining any favor with his Creator (Rom. 6:16-23; 8:7-8; Jn. 3:19). God's Word plainly tells us that it is impossible for a sinner to approach God by himself or according to his own terms.

II. Salvation Is Possible Through Christ's Death and Resurrection

A. God loved the world (mankind) so much that He did not

want man to die in his sin or to spend his life alienated from fellowship with his Creator. But as a sinner, man could do nothing of himself to bring himself into fellowship with a holy God. Sinful man only faced death, the penalty of sin (Gen. 2:17). Man needed a perfect, sinless substitute to pay the penalty for his sin in order to be reconciled to God and enjoy eternal life. "But God commendeth His love toward us, in that, while we were yet sinners, Christ died for us" (Rom. 5:8).

B. Because God so loved the world, He sent His only Son, Jesus Christ, to pay the penalty for our sin as our substitute. God's Word says, "For when we were yet without strength, in due time Christ died for the ungodly" (Rom. 5:6). The apostle Paul continues, "For if through the offence of one (Adam) many be dead, much more the grace of God, and the gift by grace, which is by one man, Jesus Christ, hath abounded unto many ... For as by one man's disobedience many were made sinners, so by the obedience of one (Jesus Christ) shall many be made righteous" (Rom. 5:15b, 19). God knew we were utterly helpless as Hell-bound sinners, and in accordance with His grace, He intervened on our behalf. He sent Jesus Christ into the world to shed His blood as the full payment for sin. In so doing, Jesus Christ died the death the sinner deserves.

C. As Jesus Christ hung on Calvary's cross, He was not dying for His own sins, for He was the perfect, sinless Son of God. He was qualified to die as our substitute because, unlike any of us, He was without sin, that is, He was sinless and incapable of sin (Heb. 4:15; 7:26). Jesus Christ was both God and man. Because He was God, He lived a sinless life, for God cannot sin. But because He was also man, He could die a physical death. He shed His blood on our behalf and bore the punishment each of us deserves. He was the *propitiation*, the "wrath-removing sacrifice," for our sins (Rom. 3:25; 1 Jn. 2:2; 4:10).

D. Jesus Christ not only died for our sin, but He also rose from the dead three days later. The Bible says He "was delivered for our offences, and was raised again for our justification" (Rom. 4:25). By His resurrection, Jesus demonstrated victory over sin and death and revealed that His work on Calvary's cross on our behalf was acceptable and sufficient in the eyes of God the Father.

III. Salvation Is Attained Through Faith Alone in the Person and Work of Jesus Christ

A. God's gift, eternal life through the death and resurrection of Jesus Christ, is a free gift of grace (Rom. 5:16-21). We certainly do not deserve to receive eternal life and a personal relationship with the all-holy God, but our Lord has made it possible for us to obtain this gift. How do we attain it?

1. Ephesians 2:8-9 says, "For by grace are ye saved through faith; and that not of yourselves: it is the gift of God: Not of works, lest any man should boast."

2. Acts 10:43 says: "To Him (Jesus Christ) give all the prophets witness, that through His name whosoever believeth in Him shall receive remission (forgiveness) of sins."

3. In John 5:24, Jesus Himself declares, "Verily, verily, I say unto you, He that heareth My word, and believeth on Him that sent Me, hath everlasting life, and shall not come into condemnation; but is passed from death unto life."

4. John 1:12 says, "But as many as received Him (Jesus Christ), to them gave He power to become the sons of God, even to them that believe on His name."

5. John 3:16-17 states, "For God so loved the world, that He gave His only begotten Son, that whosoever believeth in Him should not perish, but have everlasting life. For God sent not His Son into the world to condemn the world; but that the world through Him might be saved."

B. Clearly, then, we receive this gift by believing in the person and work of Jesus Christ. Upon realizing that we are sinners in need of salvation, we receive this free gift only through the convicting power of the Holy Spirit (Jn. 16:8-11) whereby a genuine change of mind (repentance) takes place concerning who Christ is and what He has done for us and by believing that He died and rose again on our behalf (faith). The apostle Paul preached the need for "repentance toward God, and faith toward our Lord Jesus Christ" (Acts 20:21). The convicting ministry of the Holy Spirit causes the unbeliever to understand how his sin has offended and separated him from an all-holy God. But the Holy Spirit not only thus convicts of sin and its consequences before God, but also reveals the gracious forgiveness of sin for the one who then places his faith in the Father's remedy for sin, Jesus Christ. It is God's will for all to experience this Spirit-wrought repentance (2 Pet. 3:9b). Through faith in the person and in the finished work of Jesus Christ (1 Cor. 15:1-4), we place our trust in Christ alone as our Savior from sin. We rely completely and solely upon Him, refusing to trust in *anything* or *anyone* else for our salvation. Paul says we are justified, or declared righteous in the sight of God, by *faith* (Rom. 5:1). At the very moment we truly believe, we are assured of eternal life and a personal relationship with God! The perfect righteousness of Christ is credited to our account!

C. We must understand that grace and works are mutually exclusive (Rom. 11:6). We cannot place our faith in anything or anyone other than the person and work of Jesus

5

Christ alone for our salvation and still be saved by grace. If we trust in anything, whether baptism, church membership, participation in the Lord's Supper (communion), good works, etc., in addition to the person and work of Christ, then we are not receiving God's gift of grace because we are hoping we can earn God's gift by doing something of ourselves. Grace is *unmerited* favor. As believers, we must understand and proclaim to others that salvation is only obtained by grace (God's grace) through faith. As the apostle Paul says, "If [salvation is] by grace, then is it no more of works: otherwise grace is no more grace. But if it be of works, then is it no more grace: otherwise work is no more work" (Rom. 11:6).

IV. Salvation Brings Many Benefits to the Believer

A. Fellowship With God — Believers are no longer alienated from God but are now "sons of God" and "joint-heirs with Christ" (Jn. 1:12; Rom. 8:17). We can communicate with God through prayer, and we know that He will now hear us, for we have an Intercessor, Jesus Christ, who serves as our mediator before God the Father (Rom. 8:34; Heb. 7:25;1 Jn. 2:1).

B. Sanctification — Everyone who believes becomes a "new creature in Christ" (2 Cor. 5:17). All our sins are washed away (1 Cor. 6:11), and God no longer holds our sins against us. Ephesians 1:7 reminds us that Jesus Christ has paid the price for all our sins. Those who believe in Him possess "redemption through His blood" and the "forgiveness of sins" as a result of His great grace.

C. Peace With God — Believers no longer need to fear the wrath of God that abides on all who do not believe (Rom. 1:18; Eph. 5:6). On the contrary, all who are justified by faith "have peace with God through our Lord Jesus Christ" (Rom. 5:1).

D. The Promise of Eternal Life With Christ — Although every person possesses eternal life, only those who place their faith in the person and work of Jesus Christ alone for salvation will spend a glorious eternity with God. All who reject the Savior will spend an eternity in the Lake of Fire. At the time of death, believers immediately unite with their Savior (2 Cor. 5:8; Phil. 1:23).

E. Justification — All who trust in Christ alone for salvation are declared righteous by God. The verdict is sure and eternal. The righteousness of Jesus Christ is forever credited to the account of the believer (Rom. 5:1; 8:30).

F. Empowerment to Live a Godly Life — One of the most blessed benefits of salvation is the promise that God the Holy Spirit resides in the life of every believer (1 Cor. 3:16; 6:19). It is the Holy Spirit who empowers us to have victory over sin (Rom. 8:13; Gal. 5:16), who gives us boldness to proclaim the Gospel (Acts 1:8) and who leads us into the will of God through the study of the Word of God (Rom. 8:26-27).

G. Future Glorification — All who believe will receive perfect, glorified bodies at the return of Jesus Christ (Rom. 8:18-23; 1 Cor. 15:50-54). The Holy Spirit who indwells every believer has sealed us until the day of this glorious redemption (Eph. 4:30).

Study Questions

1. What do the following verses say about the extent of sin?

   - Isaiah 64:6

   - Romans 3:10-12, 23

   - Romans 5:12

   - Romans 7:18

   - Romans 8:8

2. What do the following verses say about your state in life prior to your salvation?

   - John 3:18, 36

   - Romans 5:6-10

   - Romans 8:4-8

   - Ephesians 2:1-3

3. What do the following verses say about your state in life now that you are saved?

   - John 5:24

   - John 10:27-30

   - 1 Corinthians 6:19-20

   - 2 Corinthians 5:17

- Colossians 1:12-14, 20-22

- 2 Peter 1:3-4

4. According to John 14:6 and Acts 4:12, how many "paths" to God exist?

5. According to John 14:6 and Acts 4:10-12, what is the only "path" to God?

6. According to the following verses, how can a sinner move from death to life?

- John 3:15-17, 36

- John 5:24

- Romans 5:1

- Ephesians 2:8-9

- 1 John 5:10-13

7. According to Romans 6:23, what is God's gift to mankind?

8. What are some of the benefits of being a child of God?

9. According to Ephesians 1:7, what two things are given to those who trust in Christ as their Savior?

2

Eternal Security

One of the greatest blessings of the Christian life is the assurance that once we have truly believed in Jesus Christ and placed our faith in Him alone for salvation, we are eternally saved and secure. We cannot "lose" our salvation. While some teach that an individual can forfeit his salvation by committing certain sins or even by renouncing his faith, the Bible clearly states in several places that the true believer is securely held in Christ's hand and cannot be lost. The salvation that Jesus Christ offers is a *perfect* salvation from start to finish. Our salvation in no way depends upon our own merits or deeds but only upon the work of the Godhead—God the Father, God the Son and God the Holy Spirit. Each member of the Godhead plays a vital part in our salvation and in eternally securing us as God's children.

Before studying this important topic, it is only logical and highly beneficial to consider the fact that God desperately wants His children to *know* that they are safe and secure in Him. First John 5:13 says, "These things have I written unto you that believe on the name of the Son of God; that ye may know that ye have eternal life…." The "things" to which John refers are found in the first twelve verses of the chapter, namely, that those who believe on the Lord Jesus Christ have eternal life and, in turn, will show fruit by keeping the commandments of God as found in His Word. The apostle John wrote this portion of Scripture to "you that believe on the name of the Son of God," that is, to believers. He explains that those who are saved will produce fruit in their lives and know that they are saved. The salvation produces the fruit. In other words, fruit is a result of salvation, not a condition for it. God does not want His children to be confused or uncertain as to their relationship with Him. No, God wants us to *know* where we stand for all eternity.

I.   The Work of God the Father Keeps Us Secure

A.   Everlasting life is a free gift from God the Father — Romans 6:23 reveals that eternal life is the *gift* of God. In order for "eternal life" to be truly "eternal," it must be irrevocable, or else it would not be truly "eternal." This gift from God is obtained only through faith alone in Jesus Christ, His Son, not by any works or merits of man. Thus, the gift is entirely free. Man obtains this gift only by receiving it. The means by which it is accepted is through complete faith in the person and in the work of Jesus Christ.

B.   In His infinite power, God the Father promises to hold and protect all who have received His gift — John 10:27-30 reveals that no believer is able to be plucked from the hand of God the Father. When Jesus says that no man can pluck a true believer from His hand and that no man can pluck a believer from His Father's hand and that He and His Father are one, He is making the strongest possible statement concerning the security of the believer. No man has the ability or the power to snatch the sheep from God's hand because He is perfectly able to keep the sheep secure due to His omnipotence.

C.   God the Father promises to hold and protect the believer to the very end — Philippians 1:6 and 1 Peter 1:3-5 teach that God the Father is the Author of salvation and that, as the Author, He ensures that all His children are "kept" by

His power. Philippians 1:6 provides no room whatsoever for even the possibility that one could lose his salvation, for if such were the case, then not only would the believer not be "confident" of his salvation, but God would not actually finish what He had begun in the believer's life. First Peter 1:3-5 notes that because God is all-powerful, the believer is "kept" in the unfailing grasp of His hand. The believer has a "lively hope," or "living expectation," described in verse four. If the believer possessed the ability to lose his salvation, then he would certainly have no "hope" or confidence in the first place.

D. God the Father has promised that all whom He justifies will likewise be glorified — Romans 8:28-30 explains God's "chain of redemption": God foreknew, God predestinated, God called, God justified and God glorified. Those who have been justified are already glorified in God's sight, despite the fact that our actual glorification will not occur until the return of Christ. One's sin cannot break this chain. Those who are truly saved will not lose their salvation, for God the Father has already secured their future.

II. The Work of God the Son Keeps Us Secure

A. Because of the work of Jesus Christ on Calvary's cross, God the Father could offer to all mankind the free gift of eternal life. While our Heavenly Father provides the gift of eternal life to all who believe, God the Son made the gift possible through His death as our substitute on Calvary's cross. Romans 6:23 reminds us that the gift of God the Father is eternal life *through Jesus Christ*.

B. Because of the work of Jesus Christ on Calvary's cross, nothing can separate the believer from the love of God. Romans 8:38-39 relates this truth in the clearest possible way. The apostle Paul asks, "Who shall separate us from the love of Christ" (v. 35)? Paul's answer reveals that nothing imaginable can separate the believer from God's love which is "in (through) Christ Jesus our Lord." The Christian absolutely cannot be separated from his Heavenly Father. If we have placed our faith in Jesus Christ as our Savior, we are forever secure because nothing can separate us from God's love. John 10:27-30 also reminds us of the fact that Christ will never lose any of His own.

C. Because of the intercessory work of Jesus Christ on our behalf, we as believers can be assured that our salvation is secure.

1. Hebrews 7:25 not only reveals that we are secure once we are saved, but it also tells us how we are actually kept secure — by the interceding work of Jesus Christ on our behalf. The fact that Christ's intercession is continual reveals that although we will sin and displease our Heavenly Father at times, Jesus Christ pleads our case before the Father. Also, Romans 8:34 reminds us that Jesus Christ is currently at the right hand of the Father making intercession for us. We are forever saved due to the intercessory work of Jesus Christ, the perfect Son of God, who is accepted in the sight of the Father and who makes us to be acceptable before the Father as well.

2. First John 2:1-3 reminds us that true believers are certainly prone at times to wander from the commandments of the Word and from a right relationship with the Lord. However, we will not lose our salvation as a result of our waywardness. The perfect work of God the Son has secured our salvation, for Jesus Christ is the believer's "Advocate with the Father." God has made provision not only for the salvation of men but also for their security in Him. These verses state in no uncertain terms that John is speaking to true believers, that believers will sin at times, that when believers do

sin they have Jesus Christ as their Advocate before the Father and that a true believer will never continue in sin but will keep the Father's commandments.

III. The Work of God the Holy Spirit Keeps Us Secure

A. At the moment we trust Christ as our Savior, we are indwelt by God the Holy Spirit. The Bible teaches us in Ephesians 4:30 that the Holy Spirit seals us until the return of Christ. The Spirit is the seal of our salvation. God has already declared the believer to be "not guilty" due to the perfect sacrifice of Jesus Christ on Calvary; therefore, the seal is permanent and sure and cannot be removed. Paul reveals in Ephesians 4:30 that while it is possible for us to grieve the Holy Spirit through our actions, our sinful deeds are powerless to break the seal of the Spirit. The word *seal* in this verse literally means "to stamp for security or preservation."

B. The seal of the Holy Spirit is given to us by God the Father. Second Corinthians 5:5 tells us that God has given to us the "earnest of the Spirit." This means that the Holy Spirit is our "earnest" or "guarantee" or "down payment" by God until the very day we are glorified when Christ returns. God is the One who has sealed us, and the Holy Spirit is the seal by which we are guaranteed to be glorified one day. We are eternally secure due to the work of God the Holy Spirit.

It is a glorious blessing to understand the extent of our salvation in Jesus Christ. God has accomplished a perfect work, a perfect salvation, for He has not only provided salvation for us through the person and work of His Son, Jesus Christ, but He has provided complete security for us as well. Because He is all-powerful, He will never lose us. Because we are indwelt by the Holy Spirit, we are guaranteed to be delivered to Christ at His return.

Study Questions

1. According to the following verses, what kind of life is given to those who believe in Jesus Christ?

    *   John 3:15-16

    *   John 5:24

    *   John 10:28

    *   Romans 6:23

2. According to John 6:37, will Jesus Christ turn away any who come to Him?

3. According to Romans 8:35-39, who or what can separate the believer from the love of Christ?

4. Describe the role of God the Father in keeping the believer saved.

5. Describe the role of God the Son in keeping the believer saved.

6. Describe the role of God the Holy Spirit in keeping the believer saved.

7. The fact that we are eternally secure does not mean we have license to sin. According to the following Scripture references, what are the consequences when we commit sin as believers?

• Psalm 66:18

• 1 John 1:6-10

• John 15:4-5

• 2 Corinthians 5:10

• 2 Thessalonians 3:14

3

Baptism and
The Lord's Supper

Once an individual has trusted in the person and work of Jesus Christ alone for his salvation, he is responsible to publicly identify with Christ's death, burial and resurrection through believer's baptism. Likewise, he should also remember the death and return of Christ through the regular observance of the Lord's Supper, or Communion. These two acts are New Testament ordinances, that is, they are acts instituted by Jesus Christ that serve as an outward symbol or reminder of what Christ has done for the believer and that identify the new believer with the Savior.

It is vitally important to understand that baptism and the Lord's Supper do not serve as a "means of grace" by which an individual can obtain favor or merit in the eyes of God. Baptism and the Lord's Supper are not sacraments (that is, formal Christian rites dispensed by the church as a means of obtaining God's grace), but rather, they are ordinances that remind those who are *already saved* of Christ's work. They identify the *believer* with Jesus Christ. Salvation comes to pass only by the grace of God through faith alone in Christ's death, burial and resurrection. Yet the believer should obey the Word of God by identifying himself with his Savior through baptism, and he should regularly partake of the Lord's Supper, thereby remembering what Christ has done for him on Calvary's Cross and what Christ will do for him yet future.

I. Baptism

A. Its significance

1. Baptism serves as a picture or a symbol of the death, burial and resurrection of Jesus Christ and the believer's identification and union with Him as a part of His body. All believers comprise the "body of Christ" on earth, of whom Jesus Christ is the Head (Eph. 1:22-23; 5:23, 30). Romans 6:3-5 relates the significance of believer's baptism by stating that we are baptized "into" (that is, "in connection with") Jesus Christ. Baptism, then, is a picture, a likeness, of our identification and connection with our Savior, Jesus Christ.

2. Baptism is an important part of the life of the believer, for Christ commanded His disciples to go into all the world, preach the Gospel, make disciples and *baptize them* in the name of the Father, the Son and the Holy Ghost (Matt. 28:19-20).

B. The proper subjects for baptism

1. Only those who have genuinely believed in Jesus Christ alone for their salvation, having received God's free gift of eternal life through faith in the person and work of Christ, are proper subjects for baptism. Two reasons for this exist:

   a. Because in the New Testament, only those who *believed* in Jesus Christ were baptized with Christian baptism.

   b. Because only a believer can be identified with the death, burial and resurrection of Jesus Christ. An unsaved man or woman possesses no connection to Christ nor identification with Him but, rather, abides under the wrath of God.

2. Acts 8:35-39 reveals that baptism is to be administered only to those who have already believed the Gospel message. In this text, Philip preached the Gospel to an Ethiopian who asked, "What doth hinder me to be baptized?" Philip responded, "If thou believest with all thine heart, thou mayest." The eunuch responded, "I believe that Jesus Christ is the Son of God." Philip then baptized this eunuch on the basis of his profession of faith.

C. The proper mode of baptism

1. Single immersion (that is, the dipping of an individual under the water once) is the only proper, Biblical mode of believer's baptism for the following reasons:

   a. Single immersion is the only mode that properly pictures the true meaning or symbol of baptism. One identifies with the death, burial and resurrection of Christ by going under the water once and rising out of it once (Rom. 6:1-6; Col. 2:12).

   b. Immersion appears to be the pattern set by the early church (Acts 8:38-39).

   c. The Greek word *baptizo* from which we get our English word "baptize" requires immersion by its very definition. *Baptize* literally means "to dip" or "to immerse."

2. Any form of baptism other than single immersion cannot be considered valid baptism because it fails to accurately identify the individual with Christ's death, burial and resurrection.

21

3. A *believer* should be baptized only once for the following reasons:

    a. Such is the Scriptural pattern set forth in the New Testament Scriptures (nowhere did Christ or any of the apostles ever command anyone to be immersed more than once).

    b. Baptism represents the death, burial and resurrection of Christ which happened only once. Likewise, those who experience the "New Birth" by faith alone in the person and work of Jesus Christ experience this work of God only once in their lifetime.

II. The Lord's Supper

A. Its significance

1. The Lord's Supper, or the Communion service, is a reminder to the believer of Christ's substitutionary death on Calvary's cross (1 Cor. 11:23-25) and also a reminder of Christ's imminent (any-moment) return for His Church (1 Cor. 11:26).

2. The "bread" is a symbolic reminder of Christ's body which was put to death for us (Lk. 22:19), and the "cup" is a symbolic reminder of Christ's blood which He shed on Calvary's cross in order to bear the sins of the world (Lk. 22:20).

B. Requirements for participation

1. Only true believers in Jesus Christ should partake of the Lord's Supper. This ordinance is to be observed by the local church which should be comprised *only* of believers. Paul told the church at Corinth that he received instruction from the Lord concerning the ob-

servance of the Lord's Supper and said he delivered it "unto you," that is, to the *believers* in the church at Corinth (1 Cor. 11:23).

2. Only those believers who are walking in a right relationship with Christ should partake of the Lord's Supper. Throughout 1 Corinthians 11:23-34, Paul tells the believers that they need to examine themselves to determine whether or not they are partaking of the Lord's Supper worthily or unworthily. This means those who partake should be certain they are saved, that they are partaking for the right reason and that they are walking in a right relationship with their God. Of course, if we are harboring sin, ill-will or hatred against another brother or sister in Christ, then we are not living in a right relationship with God (1 Jn. 2:9-11). Therefore, when we partake, our consciences must be pure, and we must enjoy a proper relationship with God and with others as well.

Study Questions

1. What two ordinances are to be observed by the local church today?

2. What historic event does baptism symbolize according to Romans 6:4?

3. Who are the only individuals who are qualified to be baptized?

4. What is the proper mode of believer's baptism, and why is it the proper mode? Explain your answers using Scripture.

5. How many times should an individual be baptized? Why?

6. What is the purpose of the Lord's Supper according to 1 Corinthians 11:23-26?

7. In the Lord's Supper, what does the bread represent?

   The cup?

8. Who is permitted to partake of the Lord's Supper according to 1 Corinthians 11:27-29?

4

The Bible: God's Word

Because God desires to have a personal relationship with mankind, He has revealed Himself to us. Although man can understand that God exists by looking at creation (Psa. 19:1-6), this type of revelation is incomplete — it does not lead men to salvation or to subsequent revelation of the will of God. Therefore, God has given special revelation to man. This special revelation has come to us in the form of God's Word, the Bible. In the Bible, we can learn about God and His attributes and characteristics as well as how to have a relationship with Him and how to live a life that is pleasing to Him. Thus, the Bible is extremely important in the life of the believer.

I. The Nature of the Bible

The Bible is sometimes referred to as "God's Word" or the "Holy Scriptures." Each of these terms refer to God's written revelation to man. In this written revelation, God describes several characteristics of His Word that are essential to know and believe.

A. The Bible is given to us by God

1. The most important characteristic of the Bible is that it

was given by God. It is not just a document written by humans, but it is a divine revelation from the Creator of all things. Second Timothy 3:16 states, "All Scripture is given by inspiration of God." The word *inspiration* literally means "God-breathed." In the Scriptures, the believer possesses the very words of God.

2. Although the Bible is God's revelation to us, He used human writers as instruments who recorded the very words He wanted us to know. Second Peter 1:21 explains the process by which the Bible was inspired; it states, "Holy men of God spake as they were moved by the Holy Ghost." The writers of the Bible were "carried along" by the Spirit so that the words of Scripture are the very words of God. The beginning of the verse is also important because it shows that Scripture did not come about "by the will of man." The Bible is completely divine in origin.

B. The Bible is completely true and accurate in all matters of which it speaks

1. Another important characteristic of Scripture is that it is completely true. John 17:17 states, "Thy Word is truth." This verse is significant because the Bible is an *inerrant* (without error) revelation from God. Because our human minds are finite and our understanding is limited, the Bible may at times *appear* to contain contradictions or be difficult to understand. However, the Bible contains no errors or contradictions. Because God's Word is Truth, we can trust the Bible and know that it is reliable and accurate in all matters of which it speaks.

2. We know that the Scripture is true not only because the Bible itself claims to be true but because God, the Author of Scripture, is true. As One who is completely

holy, He cannot lie or make mistakes. To do so would contradict the very nature of God, and God cannot contradict His own nature.

C. The Bible is everlasting (eternal)

    1. Several verses teach that the Bible will last forever. Psalm 119:89, a text that describes the Word of God, says, "For ever, O LORD, Thy Word is settled in heaven." Literally, God's Word "stands firm" in heaven. It is eternally unchanging. God cannot break His promises: He cannot do that which He said He would not do, nor can He fail to do that which He has promised to do. We can be certain from now to eternity that God will keep His Word.

    2. Jesus Christ Himself referred to the everlasting nature of the divine Word. Matthew 24:35 states, "Heaven and earth shall pass away, but My words shall not pass away." God's Word will not fail. Although even the world itself will one day come to an end and be replaced (see 2 Pet. 3:7, 10 and Rev. 21:1), the Word of God will endure forever.

    3. First Peter 1:23 is another passage of Scripture that reveals to us the fact that the Word of God is eternal. It states that believers are born again "by the Word of God, which liveth and abideth for ever." Every believer can be completely assured that the Bible is the eternal and unchanging revelation from God. Everything around us may change, but what God says will always remain the same.

D. The Bible is powerful

    1. Hebrews 4:12 reveals that the Word of God is powerful: "For the Word of God is quick (living), and power-

ful, and sharper than any twoedged sword." The Greek word for *powerful* is the same word from which our English word *energy* is derived. The Word of God is powerful to accomplish its purposes. We notice the extent of this power later in this same verse when it states that God's Word "is a discerner of the thoughts and intents of the heart." Thus, the Word of God is so powerful that it is able to discern motives and to change lives. The Bible is the only book that contains such power.

2. God told Isaiah that His Word "shall not return unto Me void, but It shall accomplish that which I please" (Isa. 55:11). In this passage, God Himself is speaking in a vision to the prophet Isaiah and assuring him that His Word is powerful enough to accomplish His will. It is a comfort and encouragement to know that the power of God's Word will accomplish His purposes even though we may fail Him at times.

II. The Purposes for the Bible

The apostle Paul told Timothy that the Word of God is sufficient to fully equip the believer for effective service for his Lord and Savior, Jesus Christ. Paul writes, "All Scripture ... is profitable for doctrine, for reproof, for correction, for instruction in righteousness: that the man of God may be perfect (fully mature), throughly furnished unto all good works" (2 Tim. 3:16-17). In other words, the Bible tells us what is right ("doctrine"), it tells us what is not right ("reproof"), it tells us how to get right ("correction") and it tells us how to stay right ("instruction in righteousness"). That covers it all! Notice several purposes of God's Word:

A. For belief — One of the primary purposes of the Bible is to reveal to men the One in whom they are to believe—Jesus Christ. The Bible is God's revelation to man in order that man might believe in God unto salvation through faith in Jesus Christ. John 20:30-31 declares that Jesus did "many other signs" that are not recorded in Scripture, but God's Word says that "these are written, that ye might believe that Jesus is the Christ, the Son of God; and that believing ye might have life through His name."

B. For spiritual growth — Another important purpose of the Bible is to instruct believers so that they might grow spiritually (2 Tim. 3:16-17). The apostle Peter tells us that we should "desire the sincere milk of the Word, that [we] may grow thereby" (1 Pet. 2:2). When we grow as a result of our diligent study of God's Word, we draw closer to the Lord and better understand His love and grace (1 Pet. 2:1-3). Peter also exhorts us to "grow in grace, and in the knowledge of our Lord and Saviour Jesus Christ" (2 Pet. 3:18); the only way we know about Christ is through the Bible. Therefore, the goal of Bible study is for the believer to become mature and equipped to live a life pleasing to God as he grows closer to God.

C. For defense — The Bible also serves as an important component of the Christian's defense against sin and temptation. The "sword of the Spirit, which is the Word of God," is a part of the Christian's spiritual "armor" (Eph. 6:17). The purpose for this armor is to enable the believer to effectively stand firm against the "wiles of the devil," that is, the schemes and temptations that Satan sets in our way (Eph. 6:11). By taking heed to the Word of God, we can repel the attacks of Satan and resist the temptation to sin (Psa. 119:9-11).

D. For guidance — Another important purpose of the Word of God in the believer's life is for guidance. Psalm 119:105 says, "Thy Word is a lamp unto my feet, and a light unto my path." Although God's Word might not give us specific answers to every single question we might have, It does provide us with principles by which to live, thus serving as our guide in the midst of a dark and evil world. God's desire for the Christian life never violates the righteous commands He has given through His Word.

E. For cleansing — The Bible is like a mirror, for when we read it, we can see the areas in which we need to "clean up" our lives (James 1:22-25). James reminds us that when we look into the Bible and evaluate our lives and make changes accordingly, then we will be cleansed and blessed as a result.

III. The Importance of the Bible

Because the Bible is God's special revelation to man, it should occupy a paramount place in the ministry of the church and the life of every believer.

A. The Bible needs to be taught

1. The Great Commission of Matthew 28:19-20 reveals the importance of teaching the Word of God. The church is to make disciples of all people, "teaching them to observe all things whatsoever I (Jesus Christ) have commanded you." The truth that the church must declare is revealed in the Word of God. We need to teach the Bible to others and be taught from the Bible ourselves.

2. In 2 Timothy 4:1-2, the apostle Paul exhorted the young pastor Timothy to "preach the Word." The preaching and teaching of the Word of God is foundational to the ministry of the church and the growth of believers. God's Word is the only means by which we can know about our Savior and what He expects of us.

B. The Bible needs to be studied

1. Not only must the Bible be faithfully taught and
    preached within the confines of a local church, but it
    also must be personally studied daily by every believer.
    Second Timothy 2:15 commands us, "Study to shew
    thyself approved unto God, a workman that needeth
    not to be ashamed, rightly dividing the Word of truth."
    In this instance, the word *study* means to "be diligent."
    This implies that hard work and prayerful research is
    sometimes involved. To study the Word of God does
    not merely involve a cursory reading of the Scriptures
    but, rather, an in-depth, diligent, persistent dissecting
    of the Word of God. The good student of the Bible will
    properly handle the Word, not twisting it or misap-
    plying it as false teachers inevitably do.

2. In Acts 17:11, Paul commended the church at Berea
    because, in response to Paul's message, they "received
    the Word with all readiness of mind, and searched the
    Scriptures daily" to see if the things that Paul said were
    true. This serves as an example to all believers to be
    diligent students of the Word of God, studying it on a
    daily basis.

C. The Bible needs to be memorized

1. Although it is not easy for everyone, Bible memoriza-
    tion is a responsibility of the believer. Psalm 119:11
    declares, "Thy Word have I hid in mine heart, that I
    might not sin against Thee." It is the privilege of the
    child of God to commit His Word to memory. Scrip-
    ture memorization is profitable to the believer. One
    benefit of Scripture memorization is the defense that
    the Word provides against sin no matter where we are
    or what we are doing.

2. Colossians 3:16 admonishes believers to "let the Word
    of Christ dwell in you richly." The revealed Word of

Christ ought to flow through every aspect of the life of the Christian. The Bible needs to be learned in order to "dwell" in the believer and to have a life-transforming impact.

IV. The Finality of the Bible

A. The Bible is God's final revelation to man. God does not speak to man nor reveal Himself to mankind today through dreams, visions, miracles or other physical or supernatural means. When the canon of Scripture was complete, all temporary means of divine communication (miracles, tongues, visions, dreams, etc.) ceased (1 Cor. 13:8-10).

B. Jesus Christ told His apostles that following His ascension into heaven, He would send to them the Holy Spirit who would guide them into "all truth" (Jn. 16:13). The apostles later received the words of Christ from the Holy Spirit, and they penned these words that we now possess in the form of the Bible. The words of Scripture comprise "all truth" that we need to know for today. It alone is entirely sufficient (2 Tim. 3:16-17). No other "advanced revelation" exists or needs to exist.

Christians are to be people who read, study and memorize God's Word. We must live by the Book and hold It up as our standard for Godly living in these difficult days. It is our Guidebook, our Road Map of life. In the pages of holy Scripture, the sinner learns how to experience God's forgiveness, and the believer finds all that he needs to live a righteous life that is pleasing to God.

The importance of the Bible in the life of the believer cannot be overemphasized. In a day of subjectivity and relativism, the believer has objective, absolute truth from God. We need to make the study and memorization of the Bible a part of our daily routine so that we can be equipped and ready to live the Christian life.

Study Questions

1. According to 2 Timothy 3:16, how much of the Scripture is given by inspiration of God?

2. According to 2 Timothy 3:16-17, briefly describe the purposes of the Bible and their effect upon the believer.

3. According to 2 Peter 1:21, what Person of the Godhead was responsible for leading the writers of Scripture to pen the very words of God?

4. According to 2 Timothy 4:1-2, what is the basis of sound, pure preaching?

5. In John 16:1-16, Jesus tells His disciples He would send them the Holy Spirit following His departure into heaven. According to verse 13, what would the Holy Spirit do to these disciples?

   How does this relate to the extent of revelation available to believers today?

6. Hebrews 4:12 describes the power inherent in the Word of God. In what ways has the power of God's Word affected your life?

7. Psalm 119 is completely devoted to the subject of the Word of God. How do the following verses describe the Word of God?

    • Verse 24
    • Verse 50
    • Verse 72
    • Verse 86
    • Verse 89
    • Verse 105
    • Verse 129
    • Verse 138
    • Verse 160

8. According to Acts 17:11, why did Paul commend the Christians at Berea?

9. Explain from James 1:22-25 why the Word of God is compared to a mirror.

5

Spiritual Growth

As believers, we must understand that God wants us to continuously grow closer to Him and enjoy a personal relationship with Him throughout our lives. This is called spiritual growth. God's Word makes it abundantly clear that if we are to be the kind of Christians God wants us to be, then we need to continuously grow in our relationship with the Lord. The apostle Peter exhorts us to "grow in grace, and in the knowledge of our Lord and Saviour, Jesus Christ" (2 Pet. 3:18). Peter contrasts this growth with "being led away with the error of the wicked" and falling from our own steadfastness (2 Pet. 3:17). It has been said that every believer is either growing closer to God or wandering father away from Him. We are never stagnant or neutral in the Christian life. If we are failing to grow spiritually, then we are actually regressing spiritually.

We find the need for spiritual growth, the requirements for spiritual growth and the goal of spiritual growth enunciated in the Word of God. Just as our physical bodies need nourishment in order to grow and prosper, our spiritual inner-man also needs to be nourished with the Word of God in order for us to grow and prosper in our spiritual lives and in our walk with God. Charles Haddon Spurgeon, the great English preacher, once said, "The moment the Lord Jesus Christ saves a soul He gives that soul strength for its appointed service." The question we must ask our-selves is this: Are we utilizing the strength God has given us to grow spiritually and fulfill God's will? We must purpose to grow in the Lord each day, to become stronger in faith and in the knowl-edge of God, in order to fulfill our reasonable service to our Mas-ter. Spiritual growth is a lifelong process (Phil. 3:10-15), and we must purpose to persistently and consistently "press toward the mark for the prize of the high calling of God in Christ Jesus."

I.   The Need for Spiritual Growth

A.   First, we must grow spiritually because God tells us to do so. Ephesians chapter four commands us to "put off" the old man, to "put on" the new man and to be "renewed" in the spirit of our mind (Eph. 4:17-24). We must grow from being an unlearned unbeliever who walks according to the ways of the world into a mature believer who abides in fellowship with Christ through obedience to His Word. At the beginning of our Christian life, we should desire the "milk" of God's Word, that is, we must learn the basic prin-ciples of Christian living (1 Cor. 3:2; 1 Pet. 2:2). As we grow, we can then feed upon the "meat" of the Word and better exercise the spirit of discernment (Heb. 5:14).

B.   Second, we need to grow spiritually because we possess a natural propensity to sin, and if our sin is left unchecked, we will only wander farther away from a proper relation-ship with our Savior (Eph. 4:14, 17). Spiritual growth is a lifetime endeavor. It is a daily battle. No believer can ever reach the place in his life where he can claim to have com-pletely matured into the image of Christ. If the apostle Paul battled against the world, the flesh and the devil and needed to grow spiritually, we certainly need to do so as well (Rom. 7:17-18). Throughout the history of the human race, man has wrestled with this area of spiritual growth because man is naturally a slave to sin. Our sin nature makes spiritual growth an ongoing struggle. Yet we must never give up. We need to continually grow because, like Paul, we are in a daily battle with the world, the flesh and the devil. God's Word teaches us that our inward man should be renewed daily (2 Cor. 4:16) and should never cease from growing into the image of our Savior (Col. 3:10).

II. The Requirements for Spiritual Growth

A. Be willing and take action

1. In order to grow spiritually, we first must be *willing* to grow and to glorify God as we yield ourselves to the indwelling Holy Spirit. In Ephesians 4:23, Paul commands us to "be renewed." He did not say renewal is a natural process. Rather, it is an act of the will, and we must willingly grow and yield ourselves to God's leading.

2. Yet, a willingness to grow spiritually is not enough. We must take one step further and actually *do* it! To passively sit back and contemplate the need for spiritual growth, to be willing to grow or even to purpose to grow is not enough. While it is certainly difficult to grow at times, we must be willing to be spiritually renewed *to the point of action*. Growth and spiritual maturity can come to pass through God's enabling (Phil. 2:13; 4:13).

B. Put off the old man

1. In Ephesians 4:22, God's Word commands us to "put off" the "old man." The "old man" comprises the habits and actions of our old sinful nature to which we are naturally accustomed. Every individual possesses an old nature, a sin nature, described by God as "corrupt." We must not allow the old man to dominate our lives. Man's sin nature is fueled by lust, that is, strong de-

sires that motivate us to act in a way that is displeasing to God.

2. To "put off" the old man means to unclothe ourselves of that which is motivated by our old, sinful nature. Examples of those things which we are to "put off" include lying, wrathful anger, stealing, corrupt communication, bitterness, malice, evil speaking, fornication, covetousness and blasphemy (Col. 3:5-9). Even as believers, we will be tempted to follow the feelings of our old sin nature rather than the will of God as prescribed in His Word. Nevertheless, we must "put off," or reject, that which we know is sin.

C. Put on the new man

1. Not only must we "put off," or unclothe ourselves, of the "old man," but we must replace our clothing with something else — the "new man." In Ephesians 4:24, God's Word commands us to "put on" the "new man." The "new man" is our new nature obtained at the new birth, our salvation. To "put on" the new man is to clothe ourselves with new thinking, habits, motives and actions that were completely foreign to us prior to our salvation.

2. God's Word again gives us specific examples of that which we are to "put on." Such examples include righteousness, truth, holiness, forgiveness, kindness, meekness, patience, love, peace and thankfulness (Col. 3:10-15). As believers, our lifestyles and activities should be noticeably different than those we possessed prior to our salvation.

D. Renew your thinking

1. In Ephesians 4:23, God's Word commands us to "be

renewed in the spirit of your mind." Renewed thinking is the key to spiritual growth. The way in which
we "put off" and "put on" is accomplished only
through renewed thinking. Why? Because renewed
thinking leads to renewed habits and actions. When
we change the way we think, we will change the way
we live and act.

2. The word *renewed* means "new again." To renew our
thinking involves a complete renovation of our thought
life; it does not mean to simply combine the ideas and
philosophies of the world with those of Christ and His
Word. Our entire mind must be centered upon the
Word of God and focused upon honoring and glorifying our Savior rather than being conformed to the
world system.

3. Romans 12:2 reminds us that we can only be changed
and grow spiritually by the "renewing" of our mind.
This verse states, "And be not conformed to this world:
but be ye transformed by the renewing of your mind,
that ye may prove what is that good, and acceptable,
and perfect, will of God." The only way that we can
honor God and fulfill His will is to grow and change
spiritually, and such growth and change only results
from renewed thinking which leads to Godly habits
and actions.

E. Yield your body to God

1. In order to grow spiritually, we must yield our bodies
to God. Romans 6:11-13 commands us to refrain from
yielding our bodies as "instruments of unrighteousness unto sin," but commands us to "yield [ourselves]
unto God, as those that are alive from the dead, and
[our] members as instruments of righteousness unto
God."

2. To yield our bodies "as instruments of righteousness unto God" involves refusing to allow sin to reign in our bodies (Rom. 6:11-13). We grow spiritually when we utilize the strength and power of God to purge sin from our lives — sin does not have to dominate us (Rom. 6:14)! As Christians, we must ask the Lord to take complete control of our lives and give us the strength to do those things that honor and please Him.

III. The Goal of Spiritual Growth

A. To Exhibit Christ-likeness

1. As Christians, or "followers of Christ," our goal is to be like our Savior, Jesus Christ. How do we know how to be like Christ when we cannot physically see Him? By studying His Word to us, for everything we know about Jesus Christ and everything we know about His requirements for righteous, Christian living is contained in the pages of His Holy Word. From the Bible we can know the mind of Christ and how to have this same mind as our own (Phil. 2:4-5).

2. God's Word reveals to us that we are to be spiritually growing from the time we are saved until the day we are with Christ (Eph. 4:13; Rom. 8:28-29). This spiritual growth involves putting on the mind of Christ. How can we know the mind of Christ? First, we must be His children through faith alone in His perfect sacrifice and bodily resurrection. Second, we must be yielded to Christ as obedient children. Third, we must study the written Word, the Bible, in order to know the mind of the living Word, Jesus Christ (Jn. 1:1, 14). To be "Christ-like" involves our thoughts, motives and actions.

B. To Honor and Glorify God

1. In Ephesians 3:14-21, Paul introduces us to the way in which we glorify God — by growing spiritually and changing daily as we are "strengthened with might by His Spirit in the inner man" (v. 16). Paul concludes this third chapter by stating that the glorification of God is to be paramount in the life of the believer (v. 21) and continues in chapter four by telling us *how* we can praise God — by growing spiritually!

2. If our goal in life is to glorify God, and it should be, then we have no choice but to be growing and changing daily into men and women who are yielded to Christ, who are putting off the lusts of the flesh and putting on the mind of Christ.

Study Questions

1. According to 2 Peter 3:18, in what two areas is the believer to grow?

2. In what practical ways can we grow in grace and in the knowledge of Jesus Christ?

3. Ephesians 4:22-32 and Colossians 3:1-17 are the key passages in Scripture detailing how we grow spiritually. According to these passages, we grow by putting off the old man and putting on the new man as we renew our minds. Answer the following questions from these verses:

    What deeds of the flesh are we as believers to "put off"?

    What are we as Christians to then "put on"?

What is the key to "putting off" and "putting on" (Eph. 4:23)?

4. According to this lesson, what are the two goals of spiritual growth? Use Scripture to support your answer.

5. Paul emphasizes the lifelong process of spiritual growth in Philippians 3:10-15. In what way does Paul describe spiritual growth in verses 12-14?

6. In order to achieve spiritual growth, what must we put to death and to whom must we yield our bodies according to Romans 6:11-13?

6

Prayer

Simply defined, prayer is communication with God. Of course, as in any relationship, communication is a key to closeness and intimacy. God communicates to us through His Word, and we communicate to Him through prayer. When we fail to pray and study His Word, then we have harmed our relationship with Him, for we have closed our line of communication with Him.

Our prayers involve each member of the Godhead—the Father, Son and Holy Spirit. We are to direct our prayers to God the Father (Lk. 11:1-2), acknowledging that we are only able to access the Father through the work of Jesus Christ, His Son (Eph. 2:18). Yet, the Holy Spirit is also involved in the process of prayer as He brings to mind those things for which we need to pray and intercedes on our behalf when we do not know God's will concerning a matter (Rom. 8:26-27).

One of the best detailed definitions of prayer came from the pen of John Bunyan over 300 years ago. He wrote, "Prayer is a sincere, sensible, affectionate pouring out of the heart or soul to God, through Christ, in the strength and assistance of the Holy Spirit, for such things as God has promised, or according to His Word, for the good of the church, with submission in faith to the will of God." Clearly, prayer is an act that must not be lightly esteemed nor neglected on our part. All believers must understand what should be the content of prayer, our attitude in prayer, the frequency of prayer, some hindrances to prayer and the blessings of prayer.

I. The Content of Prayer

A. Praise and thanksgiving

1. All our communication to God should be filled with praise to Him for who He is and what He has done for us. We must remember that the very purpose of our existence is to bring honor and glory to our God. The book of Psalms records many prayers of Old Testament believers who praised and glorified God for His goodness, mercy and truth. Our own prayers should model these songs of praise. Read Psalm 103:1-22 and Psalm 105:1-5.

2. Our prayers to God should also abound with thanksgiving for His grace, mercy and bountiful blessings. The psalmist wrote, "Enter into His gates with thanksgiving, and into His courts with praise: be thankful unto Him, and bless His name" (Psa. 100:4). In the New Testament, Paul reminded the Philippian and Thessalonian believers that thankfulness was a necessary part of communication with God (see Phil. 4:6; 1 Thess. 5:17-18). Charles Spurgeon once wrote, "It is a pleasant sight to see anybody thanking God; for the air is heavy with the hum of murmuring, and the roads are dusty with complaints and lamentations."

B. Confession

1. Our prayers to God must also contain the confession of known sins. To confess our sins means simply to see those sins as God sees them; it is to recognize wicked-

ness for what it is — an affront to a holy God who cannot tolerate sin. Confession of known sin restores us to a close relationship with God whereby we are abiding in Him and enjoying His unhindered fellowship.

2. When we see our sins as God sees them and name any known sins to Him, asking His forgiveness, God promises to cleanse us of our confessed sin and even from all unknown unrighteousness that hinders our relationship with Him (1 Jn. 1:9). Psalm 32:1-5 reveals the heartache and heaviness that known sin brings to the life of the believer as well as the proper response by the child of God: "I acknowledged my sin unto Thee, and mine iniquity have I not hid. I said, I will confess my transgressions unto the Lord; and Thou forgavest the iniquity of my sin" (v. 5). God promises to restore us to a proper relationship with Him when we take care of any known sin in our lives.

C. Intercession

To "intercede" or make "intercession" for someone is to make a petition or plead with an individual on behalf of another person. As Christians, we have the wonderful privilege of communicating with God and interceding on behalf of other people — both saved and unsaved.

1. For other believers — One of the greatest privileges we have as children of God is to intercede on behalf of our fellow brothers and sisters in Christ. Such intercession reveals our love and concern for them as we pray for their spiritual, physical, financial or emotional needs. In the Old Testament, Moses interceded on behalf of the Israelites (Ex. 32:7-14). In the New Testament, the apostle Paul was a wonderful example of one who interceded on behalf of others because he cared for their well being (Rom. 1:8-12; Phil. 1:3-5; Col. 1:9-12).

2. For unbelievers — We also possess the awesome privilege and responsibility of praying for unbelievers to come to a saving knowledge of Jesus Christ. Even those who persecute us should be the subjects of our prayers. In the New Testament, Stephen interceded on behalf of those who were murdering him (Acts 7:54-60). Also, Paul told Timothy he needed to pray for *all* men (1 Tim. 2:1-4). This does not mean that Timothy was required to pray individually for every human who ever existed, but it means he was not to exclude certain individuals from his prayer list simply due to their occupation, gender, lifestyle or any other similar factor.

D. Worries and anxieties

1. As human beings who frequently suffer hardships, frustrations and various trials, we are exhorted in Scripture to bring our worries to God when we pray to Him. The apostle Peter exhorts us to cast all our cares, or anxieties, upon the Lord, for He cares for us (1 Pet. 5:7). Our great High Priest, Jesus Christ the God-man, was tested in the flesh just as we are, so He can relate to our feelings and physical infirmities and is able to help and empathize with those who are experiencing trials and temptations (Heb. 2:14; 4:15). He understands our needs and desires to strengthen us.

2. The apostle Paul reminds us to "be careful (anxious) for nothing" (Phil. 4:6). We need not worry about life's difficulties. Rather, we must communicate with God about our worries and anxieties and rely upon Him to give us His peace "which passeth all understanding" (Phil. 4:7).

E. Requests and petitions

1. Finally, the Word of God commands us to communi-

cate our requests and petitions to our Heavenly Father. We all have needs as well as desires. Sometimes, these needs or desires cause us to become worried or anxious about the affairs of this life. But Paul writes, "Be careful (anxious) for nothing; but in every thing by prayer and supplication with thanksgiving let your requests be made known unto God" (Phil. 4:6).

2. Second Thessalonians 3:1-2 is an example of a special prayer request made by the apostle Paul. He asked the Thessalonian believers to pray for him, specifically requesting that the Word of God would have "free course," or spread swiftly, and that he would be delivered from "unreasonable and wicked men."

II. The Attitude of Prayer

A. Pray boldly with faith — As we approach our Heavenly Father in prayer, our hearts and minds must be confident that He will hear us and that He has the power and ability to perform that which is according to His will. Hebrews 4:16 exhorts us to "come boldly unto the throne of grace, that we may obtain mercy, and find grace to help in time of need." It is only through our faith in Jesus Christ, our great intercessor and High Priest, that we have "boldness and access with confidence" (Eph. 3:12). So, as believers, we must draw near to Christ "with a true heart in full assurance" (Heb. 10:22).

B. Pray according to the will of God — The will of God should be the desire of our heart and the genuine motive for every prayer we utter. The Word of God clearly reveals the will of God concerning every matter of which it speaks, but James reminds us that when we bring a request or petition before God concerning a matter that His Word does not directly address, then we must always pray for God to answer our prayer according to His own will (Jas. 4:1-3,

13-15). Remember, the apostle Paul prayed that God would remove a physical affliction from his body, but such was not the Lord's will for him (2 Cor. 12:7-10). John writes, "And this is the confidence that we have in Him, that, if we ask any thing according to His will, He heareth us: And if we know that He hear us, whatsoever we ask, we know that we have the petitions that we desired of Him" (1 Jn. 5:14-15). Our Lord always knows what is best for us. If we pray for His will to be accomplished in our lives, we are assured that He hears us and will perform that which is best for us according to His will.

C. Pray in sincerity — Our prayers to our Heavenly Father must come from a heart that genuinely desires to communicate with God rather than from a heart that desires to present an outward display of pious prayers to be heard of men. Christ condemned the Pharisees for their hypocrisy and religious pretense in this matter (Matt. 6:5-8). When we pray, we must communicate with God, not with other men. Psalm 51 is a wonderful example of a prayer uttered with genuine sincerity from the heart of David.

III. The Frequency of Prayer

A. "Pray without ceasing" (1 Thess. 5:17). At no point in the believer's life should he ever cease to communicate with his Heavenly Father. To do so is to impede a proper relationship with Christ and, therefore, to deplete himself of spiritual strength and nourishment.

B. "Continuing instant in prayer" (Rom. 12:12; Col. 4:2). We should steadfastly continue to pray to God, thereby communicating to Him our praise and thanksgiving as well as our worries and requests. We should talk to God throughout the day and maintain communication with the One who gives us the strength and victory to live a life pleasing to our Savior.

IV. Some Hindrances to Prayer

A. Disobedience to the Word of God — First John 3:22 tells us that when we are obeying God's Word and pleasing Him through our obedience, then God will accomplish His will in our lives. Conversely, if we are not abiding in Christ, but rather, we are failing to obey God's Word and failing to please Him, then we cannot expect Him to answer our prayers.

B. Unconfessed sin in our life — Psalm 66:18 clearly states that if we regard iniquity (continual unconfessed sin) in our life, then God will not hear our prayer. Our unconfessed sin through the hardness of our heart hinders our relationship with God to the point that He will not even give ear to our prayers.

C. Lack of faith — Both James 1:6-7 as well as Hebrews 11:6 remind us that when we lack faith in God we cannot expect Him to heed our requests. Without faith, it is impossible to please God.

D. Mistreatment of others — First Peter 3:7 reveals that a husband's prayers to God are hindered when he fails to honor his wife and treat her with respect as he is commanded.

V. The Blessings of Prayer

A. Communion with God — Certainly all who are God's children should desire to fellowship with their Savior who paid such a great price for their salvation. Such fellowship and closeness only results from communication. When we are walking close to God and enjoying unhindered fellowship with Him through prayer and study of His Word, then we will never be uncertain as to whether or not He is hearing us and communicating with us.

B. Surety of response — We know that if we are walking close to our Lord and praying according to His will, then He will hear us. Psalm 34:15 says, "The eyes of the LORD are upon the righteous, and His ears are open unto their cry." As long as we are abiding in Him, we can be sure that our prayers will be heard and answered (Jn. 15:7).

Study Questions

1. Our prayers to God involve each member of the Godhead. From the following references, what role does each member of the Godhead play?

   • Luke 11:1-2 (God the Father)

   • Hebrews 4:14-16; 7:25 (God the Son)

   • Romans 8:26-27 (God the Holy Spirit)

2. What do the following verses say about how we are to pray?

   • Matthew 6:5

   • John 14:13-14

   • Hebrews 4:16

   • Hebrews 10:22

   • 1 John 5:14-15

3. According to 1 Thessalonians 5:17 and Colossians 4:2, how often should we pray?

4. List several possible hindrances to prayer, using Scripture to support your answers.

5. According to the following references, for whom should we pray?

   • 1 Timothy 2:1-3

   • Ephesians 6:18-19

6. According to the lesson, the content of our prayers should involve at least five things. List these five things and give a Scripture reference for each one.

7. What is the key to unhindered communion and fellowship with God according to John 15:7?

7

The Will of God

As Christians, our goal in life should be to honor and glorify our Savior, Jesus Christ. How do we bring honor and glory to Him? We do so by purposing to do that which pleases Him and by obediently yielding our hearts, minds and bodies to Him so He might use them as He sees fit. In other words, we honor and glorify our Savior by doing His will. The only way we will truly be happy is by living our lives according to God's prescribed plan and purpose for us. Those who fail to do the will of God only harm themselves and hinder a proper relationship with their Heavenly Father. All Christians should desire to accomplish God's will as revealed in His Word. Jesus Christ has even given us the Holy Spirit to lead us into knowing and understanding the will of God when questions arise in our hearts.

I.   Believers Should Desire to Seek and Do God's Will

A. Because we are new creatures in Christ, we should seek to honor the One who paid so great a price for our sins in order to set us free from sin and death. Rather than seeking to fulfill the lusts of our flesh and the desires of our own heart, the new desire of our heart must be to discover God's will for our life and live and act accordingly. The inspired words of the psalmist David should reflect our own aspirations as followers of Jesus Christ. Notice what David says:

1. We should possess a teachable spirit — In Psalm 25:4-5, David writes, "Shew me Thy ways, O Lord; teach me Thy paths. Lead me in Thy truth, and teach me; for Thou art the God of my salvation; on Thee do I wait all the day."

2. We should delight to do God's will — In Psalm 40:8, David writes, "I delight to do Thy will, O my God: yea, Thy law is within my heart." Notice the close relationship between knowing the Word of God and desiring to do the will of God.

3. We should realize that the fulfillment of God's will always leads us to righteous, Godly living. In Psalm 143:10, David writes, "Teach me to do Thy will; for Thou art my God: Thy Spirit is good; lead me into the land of uprightness." God will never lead any individual astray. The accomplishment of His will only leads in the way of "uprightness," that is, righteousness and truth as revealed in His Word.

B. Not only should we *desire* to seek the will of God for our lives, but we must *actually accomplish* His will and do it from our heart. In Ephesians 6:6, Paul tells believers not to obey those in authority over them in an effort to please men, but rather, we should obey those in authority because to do so honors Christ. Paul says we are to do "the will of God from the heart" as servants of Christ. Our motivation must stem from a desire to please God.

II. God's Word Reveals God's Will

A. Because God communicates to us through His Word, we can know His will for our lives by reading, memorizing, studying and knowing His Word. Only when we know what the Bible says can we then apply it to every area of our lives. This means that specific commands in God's Word as well as general principles for Godly living reveal God's will for our lives. Conversely, anything contrary to a command or a principle contained in God's Word cannot be the will of God.

B. Notice some specific statements contained in God's Word that reveal His will for our lives:

1. Do not mold your lifestyle after the ways of the world (Rom. 12:1-2). God's Word specifically commands us to "be not conformed to this world." Rather, as believers, our thoughts and actions must be changed as a result of the "renewing of [our] mind." Only when we begin to think and live as God desires for us to think and live can we "prove what is that good, and acceptable, and perfect, will of God." The believer is to live a holy (separated) life according to the will of God rather than to the will and desire of men (1 Pet. 4:2).

2. Keep your body pure (1 Thess. 4:3). All believers are to abstain from any form of sexual immorality. Paul specifically told the Thessalonian believers, "For this is the will of God, even your sanctification, that ye should abstain from fornication." To be personally sanctified is to set oneself apart from all sexual activity that is forbidden in God's Word (adultery, premarital sex, homosexuality, etc.) and, rather, to be set apart as one who fulfills the Word and will of Christ in regard to relationships with others.

3. Always maintain a spirit of thankfulness (1 Thess. 5:18). While we might not always emphasize the need to be thankful, God's Word makes it clear that thankfulness is always the Lord's will for the life of the believer re-

gardless of the situation in which we find ourselves. Paul writes, "In every thing give thanks: for this is the will of God in Christ Jesus concerning you." When we think about it, we have so much for which to be thankful. In fact, as Christians, we should be the most thankful people in the world!

4. Obey the laws of the land (1 Pet. 2:13-15). The Bible commands us to obey those who hold positions of authority over us. While we might not always agree with the law or with those who are paid to enforce it, believers must live as good citizens and obey the law as long as it does not conflict with the commands of the Word of God. Peter writes, "For [this] is the will of God."

5. Endure suffering for the cause of Christ (1 Pet. 4:19). The Christian life is not always easy. The Bible is full of examples of Godly men and women who were called upon to endure hardship and suffering (Heb. 11:32-40). Sometimes, it is actually God's will for us to experience times of trial and hardship. In 1 Peter 4:19, Peter says those who suffer according to the will of God must remain faithful and understand that as they yield their lives to the Lord, their faithful Creator, He will accomplish that which is best for them in their lives.

6. Be an example to other believers as well as unbelievers in speech, in lifestyle, in love, in attitude, in faith and in purity. Paul told Timothy that it was necessary for him to be an example in all these areas in order to effectively teach and witness to others (1 Tim. 4:12). This is God's will for the life of every believer.

C. Sometimes, we are called upon to make decisions concerning a particular course of action about which God's Word does not set forth specific answers. How, then, can we know the will of God?

1. We should apply principles from Scripture to the situation in which we find ourselves. For example, if we are looking for God's will regarding a good church to attend, we will look for one that meets the requirements for a God-honoring church as set forth in the Word of God.

2. Remember, it is *never* God's will for a believer to make a decision in which the results of the decision do not conform to principles set forth in God's Word.

III. The Holy Spirit Leads Us to Accomplish God's Will

A. We must never forget that the Holy Spirit, the third Person of the Godhead, indwells all who are saved (Jn. 16:7). He will direct us to the will of God if we only yield ourselves and ask our Heavenly Father to give us direction concerning issues and questions that arise in our lives.

B. In John 16:7-15, Jesus told the apostles that the Holy Spirit would guide them into all truth as the Spirit received the Word from Christ and delivered it to them. The apostles, in turn, wrote down the words of the Spirit which are now set forth before us in the Bible we possess today.

C. While the Scriptures are complete, that is, no new Scriptures are being written or inspired by God today, the Holy Spirit who indwells us continually leads us to know the truth as revealed in God's Word. Notice 1 John 2:20-27. From this text, we understand that the Holy Spirit leads the believer to know "all things," which includes:

1. The truth (v. 21)

2. That Jesus is "the Christ," that is, the Messiah who came

61

to earth and died and rose again for mankind in order to take away the sins of the world (vv. 22-23). This is the cornerstone of our salvation.

3. That eternal salvation awaits all who believe (v. 25)

4. That the believer will continue to enjoy proper fellowship with God if he holds fast to the truth (v. 24)

5. That the believer can discern between truth and error (vv. 26-27)

D. The Holy Spirit will guide us in the daily affairs of our life if we only yield to His leading and submerse ourselves in prayer, asking God to lead and guide us to do His will. As we approach God with a sincere heart and humble spirit, He will allow the circumstances of our lives to come together in a way in which His will is being accomplished in and through us.

Study Questions

1. Why should we desire to know and do the will of God?

2. According to the following texts, what are some requirements for knowing God's will?

    *   Psalm 25:4-5

    *   Psalm 40:8

    *   Proverbs 3:5-6

    *   Hebrews 11:6

3. Where do we find God's will for our lives?

4. According to Romans 12:2, what must the believer do to find God's will?

5. According to the following verses, what are some aspects of God's will that are common to all believers?

- 1 Thessalonians 4:3

- 1 Thessalonians 5:18

- 1 Peter 2:13-15

- 1 Peter 4:19

8

The Local Church and Its Ministry

All who genuinely believe in Jesus Christ immediately become part of His body, or "the church," at the moment of salvation (the moment they believe). Ephesians 1:22-23 refers to "the church which is Christ's body." This refers to *all true believers* throughout the world. These believers have been placed by the Holy Spirit into the body of Christ through their faith alone in Jesus Christ.

All believers, from the Day of Pentecost in the first century to the future rapture (or catching away at Christ's return) of the church, comprise this body of Christ. The church began on the day of Pentecost, when Christ sent the Holy Spirit to dwell within all who believed. At that very moment, a new creation was formed—the church.

The local church is the visible, outward manifestation or expression of this worldwide body of Christ. God desires that His children meet together regularly to glorify Him through study of His Word, prayer, fellowship and other acts of worship, and He has ordained the local church to be the agent through which His people organize their efforts to minister to the lost as well as to one another as they use their God-given gifts to fulfill His purposes.

I. Definition of the Local Church

A New Testament local church is an organized group of believers who are joined together and led by a pastor to worship God, study His Word, encourage and fellowship with one another, observe the ordinances of baptism and the Lord's Supper and go forth as God-ordained witnesses in the world.

II. The Purpose of the Local Church

The Bible clearly reveals the purpose of the local church through precept as well as example in the New Testament. As members of the church, the body of Christ, we need to understand what God desires concerning the purpose and ministry of the church. To fail to understand this has led many local churches into programs and practices that are not in accordance with the Word of God. We find from the Bible four basic purposes for the church today.

A. Evangelize the lost

1. In Luke 24:46-49, Jesus told His disciples to wait in Jerusalem for the gift of the Holy Spirit so they could obtain the power necessary to preach repentance and remission of sins among all nations. The disciples, who would be filled with the Holy Spirit at Pentecost and, therefore, would become members of Christ's body, needed to understand that as witnesses of Christ's death, resurrection and ascension, they were responsible for confirming the reality of the Gospel account to the unsaved (Acts 1:8). Their responsibility to the unsaved was simply to proclaim what they had witnessed and to preach repentance and remission of sins through Jesus Christ.

2. The apostle Paul reminds us that the Gospel message is spread to the unsaved through human delivery of the Word of God: "So then faith cometh by hearing, and hearing by the Word of God" (Rom. 10:17). The

only way we can "go ... and teach all nations" (Matt. 28:19-20) is to actively witness to the unsaved and proclaim the Good News to them.

3. People can be changed today only through the power of the Holy Spirit. But in order for that change to occur, we must evangelize the lost. Jesus Christ is their greatest need, and we must give them the message that will satisfy this need.

B. Instruct and edify believers

1. The role of the pastor—In Acts 20:27-31, the apostle Paul told the Ephesian church leaders to "take heed ... to all the flock ... [and] feed the church of God." Believers must be built up in the faith and instructed in the Word of God. The church pastor must fulfill his God-given responsibility to watch, warn and instruct his flock. Paul also told Timothy to "preach the Word" (2 Tim. 4:2). This "preaching" to the believers was to involve reproof, rebuke and exhortation. Jesus told Peter, "Feed My sheep" (Jn. 21:15-17). Pastors must nourish God's people. God has given us church leaders for a purpose, and that is to instruct and edify us according to the truth of God's Word (Eph. 4:11-15).

2. The role of every church member—While the leadership of the church must "feed the flock" and watch out for the well-being of the sheep, all individual believers are responsible to edify one another as well. Fellow Christians are to build up one another through encouragement and "to provoke unto love and to good works" (Heb. 10:24-25). To the church in Rome, the apostle Paul wrote, "We then that are strong ought to bear the infirmities of the weak, and not to please ourselves. Let every one of us please his neighbour for his good to edification" (Rom. 15:1-2). To the church at

Thessalonica, Paul wrote, "Wherefore comfort your-selves together, and edify one another, even as also ye do" (1 Thess. 5:11).

3. Edification and instruction by the church leadership as well as by the laity is necessary in order to fulfill the God-ordained purpose of the church. All the members of the body must contribute and work together to build up one another as they "grow in grace, and in the knowledge of our Lord and Saviour Jesus Christ" (2 Pet. 3:18).

C. Observe the ordinances

1. Baptism — The ordinance of Christian baptism pictures the death, burial and resurrection of Jesus Christ and the believer's identification with Him as a part of His body. Romans 6:3-5 relates the significance of believer's baptism by stating that those who are baptized are baptized "into" (that is, "in connection with") Christ and that baptism is a picture of our identification and connection with Christ. This ordinance was regularly observed in the early churches (Acts 2:41-42).

2. The Lord's Supper — This ordinance is a memorial, a reminder to the believer, of Christ's substitutionary death on Calvary's cross and a reminder of Christ's imminent return for His church (1 Cor. 11:24-26). Only true believers should partake of the Lord's Supper. This ordinance is to be observed by the church, which is comprised only of believers.

D. Glorify Jesus Christ

1. Because the Holy Spirit dwells within each believer, we are responsible to remember His presence within our lives and live and act accordingly. Failure to un-

derstand His place and presence in our lives brings shame to ourselves as well as to the Spirit (Eph. 4:30).

2. Because we (the church) are bought with the blood of Christ, we cannot do with our bodies as we please. We must be sure that everything we do glorifies God. Paul told the Corinthian believers that every human activity must be accomplished to the glory of God (1 Cor. 10:31). The Christian is not a law unto himself, for he is owned by Another. This principle is also certainly true concerning the activities that occur in the local church. As members of Christ's body, all our activities within our local churches must be holy and glorifying to Christ. We glorify Him through evangelism, study of the Word, prayer, singing, fellowship with other believers and observing the ordinances.

III. The Believer's Responsibility to the Local Church

All who regularly attend or are members of a good Fundamentalist, Bible-believing local church possess certain responsibilities to their church. The fulfillment of such responsibilities is necessary in order to bring spiritual growth to the believer and edification to the local church family as a whole.

A. Regular attendance — The believer who is abiding in Christ and experiencing close fellowship with his Lord should naturally desire to experience regular fellowship with other believers as well. Therefore, church attendance is something to be anticipated, not shunned. Hebrews 10:25 reminds us that we are not to forsake "the assembling of ourselves together," but rather, we are to consider and exhort one another.

B. Regular financial support — Once again, the local church is the center of ministry from which the work of God is carried forth. Such work can only proceed when sufficient funds are collected. As members of a local church, we must give back to the Lord what is rightfully His and regularly aid in the work of the ministry. Paul told the church at Corinth, "Every man according as he purposeth in his heart, so let him give; not grudgingly, or of necessity: for God loveth a cheerful giver" (2 Cor. 9:7).

C. Regular fellowship and encouragement — The believer should take advantage of every opportunity to unite with other Christians for fellowship and mutual encouragement. We need to support our church leaders and other believers by faithfully attending special church events, meetings and gatherings in addition to the regularly scheduled services. In Acts 2:42, the believers in the early church "continued steadfastly in the apostles' doctrine and fellowship, and in breaking of bread, and in prayers."

Study Questions

1. The church began in Jerusalem on the day of Pentecost. What notable events occurred on this historic day according to Acts 1-2?

2. What priorities did the believers in the early church possess according to Acts 2:42?

3. According to Romans 12:5 and Ephesians 1:22-23, who comprises the church?

4. According to Colossians 1:18 and 2:19, who is the head of this body, the church?

5. According to Acts 20:7 and 1 Corinthians 16:2, on which day of the week did the early church regularly meet for corporate worship?

6. List the four purposes of the local church and give supporting Scripture references.

7. How do the following Scripture references describe the church?

   • Ephesians 1:22-23

   • Ephesians 2:19

   • Ephesians 2:21-22

   • 1 Timothy 3:15

   • Revelation 19:7-8

8. What are the qualifications for local church leadership according to 1 Timothy 3:1-13?

9

Biblical Separation

The Biblical doctrine of separation is based on one of God's essential attributes — His holiness. By His very nature, God is completely set apart from all sin, evil and wickedness. As a result, He never looks upon any sin with the slightest degree of tolerance, and He desires for His children to likewise set themselves apart from all that is sinful and from even tolerating any form of evil or wickedness. As believers, we are called to fellowship with God who "is light, and in Him is no darkness at all" (1 Jn. 1:5). Therefore, it is absolutely necessary that we separate from whatever is "darkness," that is, whatever is in direct opposition to His very nature and His will for our lives. First Peter 1:15-16 clearly states the perfect will of God for every believer: "Be ye holy in all manner of conversation (lifestyle); because it is written, Be ye holy; for I am holy."

The belief that God is indifferent to whether or not we distance ourselves from that which His Word declares to be contrary to His will is terribly foolish and extremely dangerous. God has given us His Word so that we can know what we are to embrace and from what we are to separate. Separation from error and from those who are walking in error or those who espouse error is essential for our spiritual well-being and usefulness in service for our Lord (2 Tim. 2:19-21).

Separation from that which is contrary to the Word and will of God is sometimes difficult, but our separation from evil and every false way is always God's order. We are declared to be positionally sanctified "in Him" and are called to be separated unto Christ the moment we believe and are saved. God's Word continually admonishes us to walk in a sanctified, holy, separated manner that is worthy of our "high calling of God in Christ Jesus" (Phil. 3:14).

Although the doctrine of separation is a dominant theme throughout the Scriptures, difficulty often arises when we are called upon to actually heed or practice this Biblical doctrine. In some instances, to obey God's Word in this regard is rather easy. For example, to reject the false doctrines of the cults or to separate from an unbeliever who rejects the truths concerning the death and resurrection of Christ is not too difficult, nor does it usually involve any sacrifice on our part. However, many believers have difficulty understanding and obeying God's command to refrain from fellowshipping with those who are disobedient to the Word of God when it means they must separate from churches or Christian organizations or ministries that have compromised and failed to heed the counsel of God's Word. But God's directive for the believer with respect to evil is the same whether the sin is found outside or within the church.

I. Separation from Worldliness

A. As Christians, we have been delivered from our enslavement to sin and death. The Lord has set us free from our old masters (the world, the flesh and the devil) and has given us the power to live a life of righteousness that honors and pleases Him. So why should we desire to remain attached to the world system from which we have been delivered? The apostle John commands us, "Love not the world, neither the things that are in the world. If any man love the world, the love of the Father is not in him" (1 Jn. 2:15). The "world" to which John refers is the ungodly world system in which we live. As believers, we must not become attached to the things of the world nor gain an affinity for the world's ideas, philosophies and programs that oppose or contradict the Word of God. The Bible gives two specific reasons why we are to "love not the world."

1. Love for the world is incompatible with love for God (1 Jn. 2:15). The world system is at enmity against God and, therefore, at enmity against those who are obedient followers of Christ (Jn. 15:18-20). Notice James 4:4. Those who are friends of the world are described as enemies of God. To be an enemy of God is a serious matter! The Bible makes it clear that we cannot love the world system and simultaneously strive to effectively attain spiritual goals.

2. The world in which we live is only temporary (1 Jn. 2:17). Our present lives should reflect our spiritual priorities. If we believe the world is only temporary, then we will strive for eternal reward. On the other hand, if we live for today and attach ourselves to the world now, then we are not laying up spiritual treasure in heaven. Clamoring for material wealth and greedily striving to obtain earthly possessions is not only futile but it actually harms our relationship with our Savior.

B. Peter commands us to be obedient children of God who are "not fashioning [ourselves] according to the former lusts in [our] ignorance" (1 Pet. 1:14). This is a clear command to separate from the ways of the world in which we walked prior to our salvation. Peter continues, "But as He which hath called you is holy, so be ye holy in all manner of conversation (lifestyle)" (1 Pet. 1:15). Every aspect of our life should be conformed to the way of righteousness and Godliness rather than conformed to the philosophies and attitudes and pleasures of the world.

C. God's Word does not *specifically* (by name) forbid the believer from participating in certain worldly activities such as smoking, drug use, gambling, etc., but it does provide us with certain principles by which we are to live our lives and gauge *all* our activities. From these principles, we discover that the aforementioned activities are certainly contrary to the will of God.

II. Separation From False Teachers and False Doctrine

A. The entire epistle of Jude is an impassioned command to *all* believers to beware of false teachers who espouse false doctrine and to "earnestly contend for the faith which was once delivered unto the saints" (Jude 3). Such "contending" involves exposing false teachers and false doctrine and separating from them. We can know how to distinguish truth from error by knowing the Word of God and keeping ourselves in the love of God (Jude 17-21).

B. The apostle Paul frequently exhorts believers to separate from false teachers and the false doctrines they propagate. Notice several portions of Scripture in which Paul commands us to practice Biblical separation:

1. 2 Corinthians 6:14-18 — All believers are commanded: "Be ye not unequally yoked together (in fellowship, association or identification) with unbelievers." Instead, believers are to "come out from among them" and be separate. Any religious or spiritual endeavor (worship, evangelism, prayer, etc.) with those who have rejected Biblical truth or who preach a false gospel is a direct violation of this Biblical commandment of separation. In 1 Corinthians 7:1, Paul tells us to cleanse ourselves from all filthiness of the flesh (carnal, physical sins) and also from all filthiness of the spirit (spiritual infidelity by uniting with unbelievers).

2. Ephesians 5:11 — Paul commands us to "have no fel-

lowship with the unfruitful works of darkness." In fact, he says we are to "reprove them." We must not only separate from all groups riddled with unbelief (such as the National Council of Churches and the World Council of Churches), but we must also sound a warning to all believers who might subtly be drawn into complicity with the ecumenical apostasy so prevalent today.

3. Romans 16:17 — Paul pleads with believers to "mark them which cause divisions and offences contrary to the doctrine which ye have learned; and avoid them." Notice that Bible doctrine is the dividing line. Those who do not teach true, healthy, Biblical doctrine are to be "marked," or noted, and "avoided." As one prominent Bible teacher has said, to *avoid* these false teachers means to place *a void* between us and them.

4. 2 Timothy 2:15-23 — A heretic who denies Bible truth is to be admonished and then rejected, not embraced (Titus 3:10). A Bible believer must not find himself in common cause with such individuals, whether by ecclesiastical affiliation or in any form of joint ministry or worship. The clear call of God's Word is for every believer to separate himself from every "dishonorable vessel," that is, from those who have turned away from the truth of the infallible Word. Only then will the believer be a vessel "meet (worthy) for the Master's use, and prepared unto every good work." Only when a believer has departed from iniquity (v. 19) and has separated from those "who concerning the truth have erred" (v. 18) can he truly have fellowship "with them that call on the Lord out of a pure heart" (v. 22). If we fail to separate, the leaven of false doctrine will spread through our compromised fellowships, and, ultimately, the faith of some will be overthrown (v. 18).

5. 2 Timothy 3:1-5 — Paul describes the actions and attitudes of evil men and false teachers and warns Timothy that even though they will possess "a form of godliness," they actually deny the power of God and the Gospel message. The believer's response to these proud, conceited apostates should be to "turn away" from them.

6. Galatians 1:6-10 — All who preach a false gospel are under the curse of God, and believers are commanded to refrain from any fellowship with them. The very fact that they have perverted the true Gospel means that believers are to "let them be accursed." We are to separate from false teachers and their false teachings.

C. The apostle John also exhorted believers on numerous occasions to beware of false teachers and to separate from them and their false doctrines.

1. The entire first epistle of John informs believers that one of the primary ways in which they can abide in Christ (that is, to continue to enjoying a close relationship with Him) is to watch out for false teachers and "try the spirits" to see whether or not they are truly of God (1 Jn. 2:18-20; 4:1-5).

2. In John's second epistle, he commands us to separate from those false teachers who embrace false doctrine (2 Jn. 7-11). Those who accommodated the false teachers were described as being "partakers" of their evil deeds. The Word of God reveals that "guilt by association" is possible in the life of the believer.

D. Jesus Christ Himself commended several churches for separating from false teachers and false doctrine and rebuked several other churches for failing to separate from false teachers and their dangerous doctrines (Rev. 2:1-3:22).

III. Separation From Disobedient Brethren in Christ

   A. The command to separate

   1. Often, the most difficult type of separation to practice is separation from another brother or sister in Christ. Yet the Bible clearly states that we are to separate even from fellow brethren when they fail to heed and obey the Word of God. Some brethren embrace those who teach false doctrine. Others possess an affinity for the world and seek to employ the ideas and philosophies of the world in their lives and ministries. Some brethren actually embrace and teach false doctrine. Others repudiate certain Biblical doctrines such as separation from error and false teachers. In each case, the fellow believer is compromising the truth and failing to heed and obey the Word of God. To separate does not mean to act in an unkind or unloving manner toward the offending brethren or to refuse to speak to them or have anything to do with them. Rather, it means we must not associate ourselves with their ministries or their ministerial endeavors. We must make sure that others know we are not identified with the doctrine they teach or with the philosophy of ministry to which they subscribe.

   2. Paul commanded the Thessalonian believers to "withdraw yourselves from every brother that walketh disorderly" (2 Thess. 3:6). How were these brethren walking disorderly? They were not heeding and obeying the tradition, that is, the words and inspired writings of the apostle Paul (2 Thess. 2:15). Paul writes, "And if any man obey not our word by this epistle, note that man, and have no company with him, that he may be ashamed. Yet count him not as an enemy, but admonish him as a brother" (2 Thess. 3:14-15). Those fellow believers who do not heed and obey the Word of God

79

are to be marked and avoided. No room exists for compromise!

B. Purposes for separation from fellow Christians

1. Maintenance of church purity — Separation is necessary in the local church fellowship in order to maintain church purity. First Corinthians 5 presents a case in point, for Paul charged the church at Corinth "not to keep company, if any man that is called a brother be a fornicator, or covetous, or an idolater, or a railer, or a drunkard, or an extortioner; with such an one no not to eat" (referring to the Lord's Supper, 1 Cor. 5:11). Whether this individual was a sinning believer or an unsaved pretender, the command is the same—"purge out therefore the old leaven" (1 Cor. 5:7), that is, separate from him. When such church discipline is not enforced, unconfessed and unforsaken sin in the Christian fellowship will harm and corrupt others (1 Cor. 5:5-7). God has ordained separation in order to stem the leavening, spreading influence of sin, which always comes to pass within compromising fellowships.

2. Restoration of the disobedient brother — Unless the errant believer is rebuked according to God's Word, he might continue in his sin indefinitely. Separation should make the disobedient brother "ashamed" (2 Thess. 3:14). He is not an enemy, nor should he be treated as such (2 Thess. 3:15). One purpose for our separation from him is to bring him to a place of repentance and restoration. Paul tells us, "Brethren, if a man be overtaken in a fault, ye which are spiritual, restore such an one in the spirit of meekness" (Gal. 6:1).

3. Reception of a full reward — Believers should obey God's Word and separate from disobedient brethren in order to receive a "full reward" at the appearing of

Jesus Christ (2 John 8). We are "not crowned (rewarded), except [we] strive lawfully (that is, according to the dictates of God's Word)" (2 Tim. 2:5). It is possible for a disobedient Christian to lose reward at the Judgment Seat of Christ due to his compromised fellowships while on earth (1 Cor. 3:13-15; Rev. 3:11). Anytime a believer is identified with any religious activity that is not true to God's Word, he will meet with God's disapproval.

4. Consistency in the midst of theological confusion — Separation from disobedient brethren is necessary in order to maintain a strong, consistent testimony in the midst of theological turmoil and confusion that exists today. Compromised fellowship clouds the issues, dulls spiritual discernment and silences Scriptural reproof. Paul writes, "Be not deceived: evil communications (wrong fellowships) corrupt good manners (proper conduct)" (1 Cor. 15:33). Only a separated believer is able, in obedience to God's clear command, to sound a faithful, unhypocritical warning concerning the deception that Satan is sowing in the church today (Acts 20:28-31).

We must remember that our God is holy, and He calls us to be holy. In order to be obedient to His command, we must endeavor, by the grace of God, to be separated wholly unto Him, regardless of the cost or the scorn of man.

Study Questions

1. According to the following verses, what attributes of God make sin absolutely intolerable to Him?

   • Psalm 11:7

   • Matthew 5:48

   • 1 Peter 1:15-16

   • 1 John 1:5

2. To what does the word world refer in 1 John 2:15?

3. Look up the following verses and briefly explain why the believer should not love, or have affinity for, the world.

   • John 15:18-20

   • Galatians 1:4

   • James 4:4

   • 2 Peter 3:10-12

   • 1 John 2:15-17

   • 1 John 5:19

4. What is the basis for the believer's need to live a holy, separate life according to Ephesians 5:1 and 1 Peter 1:15-16?

5. What do the following verses say concerning our fellowships (associations) with false doctrines and false teachers?

    • Romans 16:17

    • 2 Corinthians 6:14-18

    • Ephesians 5:7-11

    • 2 Timothy 3:1-5

    • Titus 3:10

    • 2 John 9-11

6. What are some Biblical reasons for separating from a disobedient fellow believer?

7. According to 2 John 8 and 2 Timothy 2:5, what is the believer's motivation for practicing Biblical separation?

10

Relationships With Believers

Every individual who, by faith alone, has trusted in Jesus Christ as his or her personal Savior has become a "new creature," or a new creation, in Christ (2 Cor. 5:17). In addition, believers are a part of a living organism known as the *church*. In the Bible, this living organism is sometimes referred to as the "body of Christ" as in Romans 12:4-5. Elsewhere in Scripture, Christians are referred to as a "building" in which Jesus Christ is the "chief Cornerstone" (1 Cor. 3:9 and Eph. 2:19-22). As a new creation, we have become part of the body of Christ, that is, we possess a spiritual union exclusive to those who have believed in Jesus Christ. Just as a human body has many different parts, all Christians comprise the body of Christ and are spiritually united with all others who have also believed in Jesus Christ.

In 1 Corinthians 12:12-14, the apostle Paul writes, "For as the body is one, and hath many members, and all the members of that one body, being many, are one body: so also is Christ. For by one Spirit are we all baptized into one body, whether we be Jews or Gentiles, whether we be bond or free ... for the body is not one member, but many." He concludes in verse 27, "Now ye are the body of Christ, and members in particular." Clearly, all believers are united together in a special way. We are members of the same body of Christ, regardless of our culture, nationality, gender or financial status.

85

We are all "brothers" and "sisters" in Jesus Christ.

Charles Haddon Spurgeon once said, "Well may we be called brethren, for we are redeemed by one Blood; we are partakers of the same life; we feed upon the same heavenly food; we are united to the same living Head; we seek the same ends; we love the same Father; we are heirs of the same promises, and we shall dwell forever together in the same heaven."

This reality should motivate us to live as though we are a part of the same family—the family of God. Our relationship with one another should be different from our relationship with those unbelievers in the world who are not a part of this body of Christ. The Word of God has much to say about our relationships with other believers. In fact, several books of the New Testament were written specifically to address the issue of relationships between believers in the church. We must look to the Word of God as our Guidebook to reveal to us how we are to live in relationship with our brothers and sisters in Christ.

I.   Believers Must Love One Another

A.   A definition of love — The world often defines *love* in one of several ways. Sometimes, *love* is used as a synonym for "lust"; other times, it is used as a synonym for an emotional attachment to another person or object. And at other times, *love* is simply understood to mean the fulfilling of a desire. Yet the love of which God's Word speaks is entirely different from the world's notion of love. When the Bible tells us to "love one another," it is exhorting us to do whatever is necessary to advance the well-being of another individual, to have his or her best interests in mind. This love involves self-sacrifice and concern. It is a selfless love and manifests itself not by accomplishing that which the other person desires but that which is necessary for his or her well-being.

B. The Biblical command to love — God's Word repeatedly commands us to love our fellow brothers and sisters in Christ. To love them does not mean that we must agree with them in every point or issue of life, nor does it mean we must approve of their habits or even continually desire to be with them and fellowship with them. Certainly we all can think of those with whom we find it difficult to "get along." But to truly love our brothers and sisters in Christ is a command of God. We must always have the best interests of our spiritual family in mind at all times.

1. Jesus Christ told His disciples, "This is My commandment, That ye love one another, as I have loved you" (Jn. 15:12, 17).

2. The apostle Paul told the Thessalonian believers, "But as touching brotherly love ye need not that I write unto you: for ye yourselves are taught of God to love one another" (1 Thess. 4:9). This verse reveals that the desire to love our fellow brothers and sisters in Christ is placed in our hearts at the time of our salvation.

3. The apostle Peter told the believers in the early church, "And above all things have fervent charity (love) among yourselves" (1 Pet. 4:8a).

4. The apostle John wrote an entire epistle detailing the importance of love among believers. He wrote, "For this is the message that ye heard from the beginning, that we should love one another" (1 Jn. 3:11).

C. Failure to love hinders our relationship with God — It is a serious thing to have hatred in our hearts against another believer. The Bible tells us that if we do harbor hatred and fail to love another, then we are not abiding in Christ, that is, we are not enjoying true fellowship with our Savior. The apostle John writes, "But he that hateth his brother (fellow Christian) is in darkness, and walketh in darkness, and knoweth not whither he goeth, because that darkness hath blinded his eyes" (1 Jn. 2:11). Conversely, "He that loveth his brother abideth in the light" (1 Jn. 2:10). The "light" to which John refers is God Himself (1 Jn. 1:5).

D. The Biblical example of love — Jesus Christ is our ultimate example of what it truly means to love another brother or sister in Christ. We know that "God so loved the world, that He gave His only begotten Son" (Jn. 3:16). When we were enemies of God and sinners abiding under His wrath, Jesus Christ died on Calvary's cross to pay the penalty for our sins even though we did not deserve it nor even desire it. This is true, sacrificial love having our best interests in mind. "Greater love hath no man than this, that a man lay down his life for his friends" (Jn. 15:13).

II. Believers Must Edify One Another

A. The definition of edification — To *edify* another individual means to build him up through spiritual instruction or encouragement. When we edify another believer, we communicate or act in a manner in which we are truly humbling ourselves and looking out for the good of our neighbor.

B. The Biblical command to edify one another — The Bible uses the word *edify* or *edification* several times as it exhorts us to build up other believers. Romans 14:19 tells us, "Let us therefore follow after the things which make for peace, and things wherewith one may edify another." Shortly thereafter, we read, "We then that are strong ought to bear the infirmities of the weak, and not to please ourselves. Let every one of us please his neighbour for his good to edification" (Rom. 15:1-2). The apostle Paul commanded the believers in the church at Thessalonica, "Wherefore comfort yourselves together, and edify one another, even as also ye do" (1 Thess. 5:11). It is evident from the commands of Scripture that we must endeavor to build up our brothers and sisters in Christ.

C. The process of edification — How can we edify other believers? God's Word is full of information concerning how we can build up others through spiritual instruction and encouragement. Yet in order to accomplish this command, we must first put on the mind of Christ, that is, we must humble ourselves and esteem others more highly than ourselves. Philippians 2:2-5 exhorts us to "be likeminded, having the same love, being of one accord, of one mind. Let nothing be done through strife or vainglory; but in lowliness of mind let each esteem other better than themselves. Look not every man on his own things, but every man also on the things of others. Let this mind be in you, which was also in Christ Jesus." This love and humility must serve as the foundation for all our relationships. We can edify others in several ways:

1. Bear one another's burdens (Rom. 15:1; Gal. 6:2) — ask others how you can help them in their difficult times and pray with them and for them; genuine concern is the key.

2. Forgive others when they have wronged you (Eph. 4:32; 1 Pet. 4:8) — harbored ill-will or resentment in your life only serves to hinder your relationship with God and others, and such bitterness is a described by God as a destructive cancer (see Heb. 12:15).

3. Act selflessly and without hypocrisy (Rom. 12:9-10) — possess unfeigned love for others and always think about how you can serve rather than be served.

4. Warn others of that which could harm them (Acts 20:27-32) — the apostle Paul's love for the Ephesian elders

led him to warn them of the danger of false doctrine and to exhort them to stand fast in the faith.

5. Comfort one another with words from the Scriptures (1 Thess. 4:18) — sometimes, the only way in which we can comfort another is by reminding them of the truths of God's Word.

6. Speak kind words to others (Eph. 4:29) — words that reflect a heart of bitterness, wrath, anger, evil speaking and malice have no place in the life of the believer.

7. Lead by proper example (1 Timothy 4:12) — often, we can edify other believers simply by maintaining a clear, consistent witness and testimony. Our Godly example can motivate others to likewise live a life in obedience to the teaching of God's Word.

8. Maintain a cheerful countenance and heart attitude (Prov. 17:22) — Not a single reason exists for us to walk through life with a sour look on our face. We should be the happiest people in the world and, therefore, should show it on our faces and in our lives! Other believers will be strengthened and blessed as a result.

III. Believers Must Fellowship With One Another

A. Inherent fellowship — Because we have become new creatures in Christ and are members of the same body, we are automatically in fellowship with other believers in the Biblical sense of the word. The word *fellowship* in the New Testament means "that which is shared in common." All believers share the same Savior, the same indwelling Holy Spirit and the same Word of God (1 Cor. 1:9; Eph. 4:3-6).

B. Longing for fellowship — Although all true believers are technically in fellowship with one another, that is, we share the same salvation in Christ, we are not always actively involved in physical fellowship with other believers. In some cases, fellowship is not possible because another believer has broken the fellowship by disobeying the Word of God. At other times, we might find ourselves far removed from a local body of believers with whom we can fellowship in good conscience. And yet other times, we do belong to a good, Bible-believing church but willfully refrain from enjoying the fellowship of fellow believers of like precious faith. Why is this so? As Christians, we should naturally desire to fellowship with other believers, a desire that we did not possess prior to our new birth. Acts 2:42 provides a good example of the way in which we can fellowship with one another. We can, in good conscience, fellowship with other believers today in the following ways:

1. Gather around the teaching, preaching or studying of the Word of God as it is faithfully and truthfully delivered.

2. Unite with others of like heart and mind around the Lord's table.

3. Pray with one another, bringing petitions, praises and intercessions before the Throne of Grace.

4. Spend time together in any location or in any circumstance discussing all the wonderful works of God and growing closer as brothers and sisters in Christ.

It is evident from God's Word that our relationships with other Christians must always be marked by love, edification and fellowship. So much strife and division within the body of Christ could be avoided if every Christian did his part to love others, edify others and fellowship with members of Christ's body.

Study Questions

1. What terms are used in the following verses to describe the believer's unity with fellow believers?

   • Romans 12:4-5

   • Ephesians 2:19

   • Ephesians 2:21

   • Revelation 19:7-8

2. Describe the kind of love that believers are to have for one another.

3. Read Philippians 2:2-5 and describe how the believer who has the "mind of Christ" will treat other believers.

4. According to the following verses, what are some ways we can edify other believers?

   • Romans 15:1

   • Ephesians 4:32

- 1 Peter 4:9

- Acts 20:31

- 1 Thessalonians 4:18

- Ephesians 4:29

- 1 Timothy 4:12

- Proverbs 3:27

5. What is the foundation for believers' fellowship with one another according to 1 Corinthians 1:9?

6. According to 2 Thessalonians 3:6, what is one reason for discontinuing fellowship with a fellow believer?

7. List some ways in which believers can fellowship with each other.

11

Relationships With Unbelievers

All who have believed in Jesus Christ have become new creatures (2 Cor. 5:17). This means they have a new family, a new heart, a new mind and a new God. Their priorities are different, their goals are different and their lifestyles are different than they were prior to their new birth. Yet all believers still live in this same old evil world. We are surrounded by millions of people who have not become new creatures in Christ, and their priorities, goals and lifestyles are different than ours. God's Word commands us to live peaceably with the unbelievers around us and seek for opportunities to witness to them while simultaneously refusing to participate in or embrace their behavior, philosophies and lifestyles. God's Word provides us with several principles that should guide us in our relationships with those who do not know Jesus Christ as their Savior.

I. Build Positive Relationships With All People

A. Befriend unsaved people

1. In order to be "Christ-like," it is imperative that we act friendly and cordial toward those who are unsaved. Jesus Christ never acted in a rude or unkind manner toward anyone, regardless of whether they believed

in Him as the Messiah, rejected Him or only appreci-
ated Him for the miracles and healings He performed.
In His day, Jesus Christ was known as "a friend of
publicans and sinners" (Matt. 11:19).

2. Proverbs 18:24 reminds us that "a man that hath friends
   must shew himself friendly." We can often be more effective witnesses for Christ to those who are our own
   friends, and in order to have friends, we must be cordial and friendly.

B. Love unsaved people — Just as God so loved the world
   (all unsaved people), so we, too, are to love the unsaved
   and possess a burden to see them come to Christ. In 1 Thessalonians 3:12, Paul prays that God would make the believers to "increase and abound in love one toward another, and toward all men." Our love for unbelievers
   should motivate us to be concerned for their well-being
   and to tell them the Good News.

C. Do good to all men — In Galatians 6:10, Paul exhorts us,
   "As we have therefore opportunity, let us do good unto all
   men." He also tells us that rather than being vengeful and
   rendering evil for evil when we are wronged, we should
   "follow that which is good ... to all men" (1 Thess. 5:15).

D. Live peaceably with all men — Believers should never at-
   tempt to pick a fight with the unsaved or be antagonistic
   in any manner. On the contrary, we are commanded to "follow peace with all men and holiness" (Heb. 12:14) and "live
   peaceably with all men" (Rom. 12:18). We can do our part
   to live peaceably by displaying an attitude of meekness
   and humility rather than pride and boastfulness (Titus 3:2).

E. Honor all men — Despite the sinful behavior and mis-
   placed devotion of the unsaved, we are commanded to
   "honor all men" (1 Pet. 2:17). We show honor by respect-

ing them, loving them and treating all individuals as equals.

F. Be patient with unbelievers — Paul tells us in 1 Thessalonians 5:14 to "be patient toward all men." God can work in the hearts of the unsaved, and He can work in ours as well as we strive to patiently proclaim the truth and allow the Holy Spirit to convict them of their sin and need for a Savior.

G. Pray for the unsaved — Paul told Timothy, "I exhort therefore, that, first of all, supplications, prayers, intercessions, and giving of thanks, be made for all men ... for this is good and acceptable in the sight of God our Saviour" (1 Tim. 2:1, 3). Unbelievers should never be excluded from our prayers. We are responsible to pray for their salvation.

II. Find Opportunities for Witness

A. Live an exemplary lifestyle

1. If we live as followers of Christ in this evil, sin-cursed world, we will certainly stand out from the crowd, and, as a result, we will gain opportunities to witness to those who ask us why we are different.

2. Paul exhorted Timothy to be "an example of the believers." He was to model God's will for the believer's speech, behavior, love, attitude, faith and purity (1 Tim. 4:12). Titus was also commanded to demonstrate his life as "a pattern of good works" (Titus 2:7). We, too, must live exemplary lives if we desire to honor Christ and be a testimony to those around us of His saving, life-changing power.

B. Communicate the Gospel to unbelievers

1. Not only must we live an exemplary life, but we must also proclaim the Gospel to the unsaved. No individual can come to Christ by merely observing our conduct and lifestyle. We know that "faith cometh by hearing, and hearing by the Word of God" (Rom. 10:17). We are responsible to tell the unsaved about the hope that is within us (1 Pet. 3:15).

2. The apostle Paul declares that through the preaching of the Gospel individuals are saved (1 Cor. 1:21). As a result, their lives are changed (Eph. 2:1-9). We cannot expect our friends, relatives or acquaintances to experience the new birth without explaining to them the Good News concerning the person and work of Jesus Christ.

C. Be accessible to unbelievers

1. As we build friendships with those friends, neighbors and relatives who do not know Christ, we must make them aware that we are always accessible and willing to speak to them about any matters that arise in their lives. If they feel that we are too busy to give them our time or if they think we do not truly care about their concerns and problems, they will not feel as though they can comfortably approach us when they desire to discuss spiritual matters.

2. In the New Testament, the apostle Paul is a good example of one who was always accessible to those who desired to hear the Gospel. Likewise, Jesus Christ Himself always responded to those who sought to hear His message (Jn. 3:1-3).

III. Do *Not* Participate in Worldly Behavior

A. As Christians, we must remember that we are *in* the world but not *of* the world. We are only strangers and pilgrims here on this earth. Our true citizenship is in heaven. Therefore, our lives should not conform to the world in which we live.

1. While we must always be prepared to do good to all men and find opportunities to witness to them, we must never compromise our Biblical convictions nor partake in worldly activities with the unsaved that would identify us with the wickedness of the world rather than with Jesus Christ. We must remember that "the wisdom of this world is foolishness with God" (1 Cor. 3:19). Therefore, we must act and think according to the mind and will of God rather than to the ways and philosophies of the world and those who embrace this world.

2. Jesus Christ told His disciples that the world did not love them because they were not of this world but, rather, He had chosen them out of the world (Jn. 15:19). Likewise, while we live in this world, we are not of this world and have been chosen "out of" this world. Therefore, we must not live as though we are of this world. In 1 John 4:5-6, the apostle John contrasts those who are "of the world" with those who are "of God." Those who are "of the world" possess a love for the world system and an affinity toward the pleasures and philosophies of the world. Conversely, those who are "of God" listen to the words of the apostles, which, through inspiration, are the very Words of God.

B. We must not be a stumblingblock to others

1. A Christian who magnifies his regard for the world higher than his love for his Savior not only jeopardizes his own relationship with God but may also act as a stumblingblock to others. For example, an unbeliever

might see a Christian living a worldly lifestyle and question why he would even need to trust in Christ when he already has so much in common with his "Christian" friend. Likewise, a believer might see another believer living like the world and wonder why he should not act in such a manner as well, even though it appears as though God's Word requires righteous and Godly living. In either case, holiness is disregarded, and an individual's growth is hindered.

2. When a question arises as to whether or not a particular activity is suitable for the believer, it is usually wise to take the safe route and refrain from indulgence or participation in order to avoid being a stumblingblock to someone else. Romans 14:13-18 refers to this matter and concludes, "Let us therefore follow after the things which make for peace, and things wherewith one may edify another" (Rom. 14:19). In addition, Paul told the Corinthians that the believer must never allow his liberty in Christ to become a stumblingblock to others (1 Cor. 8:9).

As Christians, we must remember that we cannot serve two masters (see Matt. 6:24 and Jas. 4:4). It is impossible for us to love the world and live like the world and simultaneously love our Savior and live a life that is honoring and pleasing to Him. Although we must love unsaved people, befriend them, be accessible to them and share the Gospel with them, we must remember that we are called to a life of holiness and righteousness, and it is imperative that we honor and glorify God by living accordingly.

Study Questions

1. According to 1 John 4:8-11, who is the believer's example concerning how to treat the unsaved?

2. If an unbeliever taunts or verbally attacks a believer, what is to be the believer's response according to the following verses?

   • Romans 12:17-18

   • 1 Thessalonians 5:15

   • Hebrews 12:14-15

3. According to the following verses, what is to be the believer's attitude toward government or other authority figures, whether they are saved or not?

   • Matthew 22:19-21

   • Romans 13:1-7

   • 1 Peter 2:13-18

4. According to 1 Timothy 4:12, in what six areas are we to be an example "of the believers"?

5. What does 1 Peter 3:15 command the believer concerning opportunities for witness?

6. According to the following verses, why is it necessary to witness to unbelievers?

   • Mark 16:15

   • Acts 4:12

   • Romans 10:17

   • 1 Corinthians 1:21

7. Why is the popular philosophy of becoming "like the world in order to win the world" wrong according to the following verses?

   • Romans 6:1-2

   • 1 Corinthians 8:9

   • 1 John 2:15-16

12

Relationships
in the Workplace

Many of us spend most of our waking hours at our place of employment. Usually, one third of our day is spent at work in order to earn a living for ourselves and our families. Due to this fact, we must understand the Biblical guidelines for proper relationships in the work place. God's Word gives explicit instructions to both employers as well as employees concerning proper behavior and attitudes in the work place. While these portions of Scripture specifically refer to the bondservant/master relationship that was so prevalent in the first century, these basic principles apply to all of us today who serve as either employers or employees in our various occupations.

Regardless of whether those with whom we work are believers or unbelievers, we are responsible to follow Biblical guidelines in our interaction with our colleagues. Likewise, it does not matter whether or not we really enjoy our jobs, our bosses, our employees or our co-workers — we are still required to obey the Word of God concerning our relationships with others, regardless of how we feel about our situation. If we obey God's Word, we will honor and glorify our Lord, and we will serve as vibrant witnesses to the Truth to those around us. After all, our goal in life is to be more like our Savior and to glorify Him in everything we do! God's Word addresses the responsibilities of the employer to the employee, the responsibilities of the employee to the employer and the responsibilities of employees to one another. The following texts reveal God's will concerning our relationships in the workplace: Ephesians 6:5-9; Colossians 3:22-4:1; 1 Timothy 6:1-2; Titus 2:9-10 and 1 Peter 2:18-19.

I. The Responsibilities of the Employer to the Employee

A. An employer must treat all employees with respect.

1. Those who are in a position of authority in the workplace are to treat their employees as they themselves would want to be treated. In Ephesians 6:9, the apostle Paul emphasizes this truth when he says, "And, ye masters, do the same things unto them (the bondslaves)."

2. In Ephesians 6:9, Paul also reminded those in authority, "Neither is there respect of persons with [God]." Employers, managers, supervisors or others in positions of authority are to remember that just as God is not a respecter of persons, neither should they be partial regarding their employees. All should be treated with equal respect.

B. An employer must communicate with all employees in an edifying manner.

1. Again, in Ephesians 6:9, the apostle Paul commands those who are in authority to refrain from threatening those who are under them. While it may be difficult at times to deal with an employee in an edifying, rational manner, such complicated situations never warrant disobedience to the Word of God.

2. Ephesians 6:9 also reveals the believer's motivation for communicating with employees in an edifying man-

ner: "Knowing that your Master also is in heaven." All who possess authority on earth are under the authority of One who is greater. Our loving Father never threatens His own, but communicates in love and forbearance. All believers should emulate this approach.

C. An employer must never take advantage of his or her employees.

1. In Colossians 4:1, Paul commands those in a position of authority to "give unto your servants that which is just and equal; knowing that ye also have a Master in heaven." It is evident from the words of Scripture that those in authority are to treat employees in a fair and just manner. This involves an appropriate wage as well as necessary rest and benefits. An employer must never cheat his workers or refrain from giving them fair and equitable compensation.

2. Once again, notice that the motivation for such behavior is the example of the Lord Jesus Christ (Col. 4:1). The believer has no right to cheat or take advantage of others when he himself is treated fairly and justly by his own Lord and Savior, even though he does not deserve to be treated in such a kind manner.

II. The Responsibilities of the Employee to the Employer

A. Employees must always treat their employers with respect.

1. Regardless of how respectable an employer may or may not be, believers are to treat those in authority over them with respect. This is a Biblical command. In fact, Timothy was specifically commanded to teach believers to "count their own masters worthy of all honour" (1 Tim. 6:1). While the temptation to "talk back" to those in authority or to belittle them behind

their backs is sometimes great, believers must not give in to such fleshly desires. Paul even told Titus that servants were to obey their masters, "not answering again" (Titus 2:9).

2. Why is it necessary to treat even an unjust or unreasonable employer with respect? Because God's Word commands it, and to do otherwise blasphemes the name and doctrine of God (1 Tim. 6:1). Our Christian testimony is often ruined when we treat others with a lack of respect.

B. Employees must obey their employers.

1. God's Word continually commands bondservants to obey their masters. Read Ephesians 6:5-8, Colossians 3:22-25 and Titus 2:9-10. Throughout these passages, the employee is exhorted to obey his employer. Regardless of whether the assigned task is simple or difficult, enjoyable or tedious, prestigious or humiliating, believers must fulfill the duties imposed by those in authority over them.

2. Believers are to obey their employers "as unto Christ ... doing the will of God from the heart" (Eph. 6:5-6). They are to obey "not with eyeservice, as menpleasers; but in singleness of heart, fearing God" (Col. 3:22). In other words, obedience should result from a proper motivation for service. We should serve and obey those over us because to do so brings honor and glory to God as well as future reward to the believer for faithful, obedient service while on earth (Col. 3:23-24).

C. Employees must never cheat their employers.

1. Those who obey their employers and demonstrate an attitude of respect for them will certainly give them an

honest day's work for an honest day's wage. It is evident that our attitude determines our actions. Paul commands believers to work hard and to not be "slothful in business" (Rom. 12:11). Proverbs 13:11 tells us that the Biblical way in which we gain the money necessary to meet our needs is through hard work. Cheating one's employer or obtaining money through dishonest means is an offense to God.

2. Titus 2:10 commands the employee to refrain from any form of stealing or petty theft. Rather, the employee should show "all good fidelity," that is, he should be trustworthy, faithful and honest in every aspect of his job. Why? Because, as Paul reminds Titus, to be honest and trustworthy is to "adorn the doctrine of God." Our Savior commands us to "put off" lying, cheating and stealing, among other sins. The employee who heeds this teaching, or doctrine, is clearly showing himself to be a faithful, obedient servant of Christ.

III. The Responsibilities of Employees to One Another

A. Employees must show respect to one another — Regardless of whether we are working with believers or unbelievers, we must treat our co-workers with respect and impartiality. Failure to do so will only bring tension in the workplace as well as reproach to the cause of Christ. The apostle Paul writes, "As much as lieth in you, live peaceably with all men" (Rom. 12:18). We can do our part to live and work peacefully with others by being respectful to them.

B. Employees must not be vengeful or vindictive toward those who offend them — While we might try our hardest to respect others and live peaceably with them, we will often come into contact with those who are bitter, selfish or vindictive. Our response should be to maintain a Christian attitude toward the offender and simply allow God and others in authority to handle this person in the proper way at the proper time. God's Word commands us to "recompense to no man evil for evil" and to avenge not ourselves but rather to "overcome evil with good" (Rom. 12:17, 19, 21).

Study Questions

1. According to Ephesians 6:9, how does God expect employers to treat their employees?

2. According to Ephesians 6:9 and Colossians 4:1, why are employers to treat those under them in a proper manner?

3. What is God's standard for how much an employer is to compensate his worker according to Colossians 4:1?

4. Why are employees to honor (respect) their employers (1 Tim. 6:1)?

5. According to the following verses, how is the employee to respond to an assignment that he does not want to do (assuming the task does not require one to sin)?

• Ephesians 6:5

• Colossians 3:22

• Titus 2:9

6. According to the following verses, how are employees to view their work?

• Ephesians 6:5-7

• Colossians 3:23-24

• 1 Corinthians 10:31

7. What does Romans 12:11 tell us concerning the way in which we are to accomplish our work?

13

Relationships in the Home

Since the creation of man, God has established the institution of marriage. And since the creation of man, Satan has sought to destroy this institution by sabotaging the relationships within the family unit. Half of all marriages today end in divorce. Men are forsaking their wives and children for their jobs or other attractions. Children have no respect for their parents and fail to be brought under their control. Women are ruling over their husbands and their homes as though they were the final authority in all family matters. Few, if any, need to be convinced that today's families are in a real mess. Satan is turning families upside down and inside out. He hates God's family plan and wants to see it fail miserably.

God, on the other hand, has set forth His will concerning our place and our responsibilities in the home. The world hates God's model, but because our Creator knows what is best for us, we must look into His Word to discover His will for our relationships in the home.

God's plan for the family is centered in His very creation of man and woman. Today, Christians and unbelievers alike must realize the difference between equality and function in the home in order to understand God's role for men and women in the marriage relationship: Both men and women are equal in God's eyes, yet they possess different functions in the home and family.

Read Genesis 1:26-28 and Genesis 2:15-25. From these texts we learn that men and women are created as equal persons but possess different functions in the home. Equality between the sexes is revealed in the following ways: Man and woman are both made in the image of God (vv. 26-27); the man and woman were both to have dominion over the earth (v. 28); and, the woman was created to be a helper "meet" or "comparable," "suitable" or "fitting" for man (2:18). This means she was a "counterpart" to him. Yet these texts also reveal the difference in the roles, or functions, of the sexes. The woman was to be a "helper" to the man (2:18). Also, the curse God pronounced upon each was different, revealing a difference in function (3:16-19). From these verses we see that God had already set boundaries and differences in function.

Since the fall, man's selfish, sinful nature has continually served as a hindrance to the peace and unity God desires in the relationships between man and woman. According to Genesis 3:16, a sinful power struggle now plagues the home. The wife desires to usurp authority, and the intensity of man's ruling adds conflict as well. Still today, man and woman are equal as individual persons in the sight of God, yet they possess different functions in God's economy. In order to live as the Lord would have us to live, our role as Christians is to conquer the sinful nature that seeks to destroy and ruin our relationships and proper functions in the home. How do we do this? Only through the power of the Spirit, as we walk according to the Spirit. The demonstration of the filling of the Spirit manifests itself in our relationships with one another, specifically in the home. The husband, wife and children all possess distinct roles and functions within the family unit.

I. The Role of the Husband

A. The husband is to possess headship over his wife (Eph. 5:23).

1. What is headship? It can be defined in the following way: Headship is authoritative leadership, as demon-

strated by Jesus Christ Himself, which purposes to bring honor and glory to Christ and the edification of all involved. Headship is not "dictatorship" but simply "authoritative leadership."

2. It is important to understand that this headship seeks the best interests of all involved when decisions need to be made (Eph. 5:28-29). The husband is to make decisions that benefit the entire family, not just himself.

B. The husband is to love his wife (Eph. 5:25; Col. 3:19).

1. If the husband truly loves his wife and demonstrates his love for her as he should, he will always have her best interests in mind, just as Jesus Christ loves us and always has our best interests in mind.

2. This Greek word for love (*agapeo*) not only denotes a sacrificial love that always bears in mind the best interests of another, but it also refers to a purifying love (Eph. 5:26-27). The wife should be a better Christian and have a closer relationship with God, her husband and her family as a result of her husband. Husbands must ask themselves, "Is my wife more like Christ because she is married to me? Am I causing her to be a better wife and mother, or am I holding her back from the best Christ has to offer her?"

C. The husband is to reverence and respect his wife (1 Pet. 3:7).

1. Reverence and respect are natural results of love. To reverence and respect the wife means the husband's actions result from an understanding of his wife. *Knowledge* in 1 Peter 3:7 means "to know experientially." A husband must spend time with his wife, getting to know her likes and dislikes and doing that which

pleases her while refraining from doing that which displeases her.

2. This respect and reverence should mirror the fact that both man and woman are equal in the eyes of God. Both the husband and wife who know Jesus Christ as their personal Savior are "heirs together of the grace of life."

II. The Role of the Wife

A. The wife is to submit to the headship of the husband (Eph. 5:22, 24; Col. 3:18; 1 Pet. 3:1; Tit. 2:5).

1. To *submit* or demonstrate "submission" does not denote inferiority. Rather, to submit means to recognize one's role or function and act accordingly.

2. It is contrary to Scripture and God's plan for mankind in general for the wife to serve as the final authority in the home. She must recognize the fact that God has placed the husband in a position of leadership. While open communication and compromise are often necessary in any relationship, when a final decision needs to be made concerning a matter on which the husband and wife cannot agree, God has commanded the husband to make the final decision and the wife to respect the husband's authority to make that decision.

B. The wife is to reverence her husband (Eph. 5:33). To "reverence" means to respect someone by recognizing his position. The wife should respect her husband by acknowledging his role as the head of the house, by treating him as an equal in the eyes of God, by refraining from gossiping or speaking negatively about him to others behind his back and by recognizing him as a partner in the marriage covenant and loving him accordingly.

C. The wife is to love her husband (Titus 2:4). She must demonstrate the same sacrificial love for him that he is to demonstrate toward her.

D. The wife is to beautify herself through her actions and attitudes (1 Pet. 3:1-4). Rather than focusing primarily upon attaining physical beauty in the effort to gain the world's attention and approval, the Godly wife will reveal her true beauty by living an exemplary life and possessing an attitude that conforms to the Word and will of God.

III. The Role of the Parents

A. The father (Eph. 6:4; Col. 3:21)

    1. The father must not provoke his children to wrath or anger. This entails unnecessary or excessive words or actions on the part of the father that bring undue discouragement to the child or a feeling of hatred toward his parents.

    2. The father, rather, must bring his children up in the nurture and admonition of the Lord. This means he must teach his children to do right, and he must discipline them in a loving manner when they do that which is wrong. Such chastening should be accomplished in the same spirit in which our perfect Heavenly Father chastens us (notice Prov. 13:24 and Prov. 29:17).

B. The mother (1 Tim. 5:14; Titus 2:4-5)

    1. The mother must love her children (Titus 2:4). This love involves self-sacrifice at times. It includes reproof and rebuke when the children do that which is harmful as well as praise and affirmation when the children do that which is right.

2. The mother is to guide and manage the affairs of the house and refrain from idleness which only leads to sinful habits and actions (1 Tim. 5:13-15 cf. Titus 2:4-5).

IV. The Role of the Child (Eph. 6:1-3; Col. 3:20)

A. Obey your parents — To *obey* literally means, in this text, "to get under the authority of" the parents by listening to them and heeding their instructions. This obedience has been defined as "the foundational interpersonal relationship for a healthy society." When children are taught to obey the authority of their parents and respect them and their God-ordained position, they will not find it difficult to obey and respect other authority figures throughout their lives.

B. Honor your parents — This has to do with one's attitude. Children must respect, love and care for their parents throughout their lives. Parents may not always fulfill their role in the Godly manner in which they should, but children must still honor them as their parents.

Study Questions

1. When were the functions (roles) of husband and wife established?

   When did problems arise concerning these roles?

2. What does "headship" in the home entail, and who is to have the headship in the home according to Ephesians 5:23?

3. What visible and non-visible results occur when husbands love, reverence and respect their wives?

   What visible and non-visible results occur when wives love, reverence and respect their husbands?

4. Why is the wife to "submit" to her husband?

5. What does Ephesians 5:33 mean when it says the wife is to "reverence" her husband?

6. What are the father's Biblical duties concerning his children?

What are the mother's Biblical duties concerning her children?

7. Explain the role of the child in the home.

14

New Testament Giving

Many Christians do not consider giving to be one of the great important truths or tenets of the Christian faith, but the doctrine of giving is one of the most important foundations upon which our Christian faith is built. In 1 Timothy 2:5-6, the apostle Paul reminds us that Jesus Christ "gave Himself a ransom for all." Our own salvation rests upon the fact that Jesus Christ gave something to us. He gave us His own life. In John 3:16 we read that "God so loved the world, that He gave His only begotten Son." God the Father gave us His Son, who fulfilled His Father's will by laying down His life, giving Himself to us as "a ransom for all." In 2 Corinthians 8:9, Paul tells us, "For ye know the grace of our Lord Jesus Christ, that, though He was rich, yet for your sakes He became poor, that ye through His poverty might be rich." What a wonderful, incredible gift!

When we truly understand the importance of giving and the price paid for our own salvation, we will be more thankful for the gifts given to us and will purpose to follow our Savior's example by giving back to Him. Our Lord and Savior, Jesus Christ, has given so much to us. In fact, everything we possess rightfully belongs to Him, and He has merely entrusted it to us as His stewards. James writes, "Every good gift and every perfect gift is from above, and cometh down from the Father of lights" (James 1:17). Therefore, all believers should give their time, money, effort and talent back to their wonderful Lord. Because believers have received everything they possess from the hand of their Heavenly Father, all believers should practice regular giving. To give back to God is not the responsibility of only certain believers; rather, it is expected of all saints whether they be rich or poor. The Word of God gives us instruction concerning the need for giving, principles regarding the amount to give and commandments relating to our attitude toward giving.

I.   The Need for Giving

A.   Everything we possess already belongs to God.

1.   Psalm 24:1-2 reminds us that "the earth is the LORD's, and the fulness thereof; the world, and they that dwell therein. For He hath founded it upon the seas, and established it upon the floods."

2.   We are only stewards of that which has been entrusted to us. The problem that exists today is this: Many Christians are not practicing good stewardship. Like many unbelievers, they are spending money they do not have for things they do not need in order to impress people they do not even like.

B.   Giving is commanded in God's Word.

1.   Just as the believer is commanded by God to abound in faith, speech, knowledge, diligence and love, so he is likewise commanded to abound in the grace of giving (2 Cor. 8:7). The act of giving proves the sincerity of the believer's love for the Lord and for His work (2 Cor. 8:8). Therefore, giving is a way of expressing our love for God.

2.   The apostle Paul informs the believer that he should

give to the Lord as he has purposed in his own heart. He writes, "Every man according as he purposeth in his heart, so let him give" (2 Cor. 9:7). Paul told the church in Corinth that they were each to set aside a certain amount of money that God had led them to give and place that money in the hands of the church each Sunday (1 Cor. 16:1-2).

C. Financial giving supplies the needs of the ministry.

1. God accomplishes many of His purposes through the offerings of the saints. In order for a local church to function Biblically, church leaders must be paid, church bills must be paid and church ministries must be funded. If God's people fail to give back to Him through their offerings to the local church, the ministry of the Word will be hindered.

2. Financial giving is not only God's way of meeting the needs of the local church but also God's way of meeting the special needs of believers who are doing the work of the Lord elsewhere. In 1 Corinthians 16:1-4, such giving aided the suffering church in Jerusalem. In Philippians 4:14-19, financial giving allowed the temporal needs of the apostle Paul to be met. This giving was described as "an odour of a sweet smell, a sacrifice acceptable, wellpleasing to God" (Phil. 4:18). Paul reminded the believers that God provides for those who put the needs of His work first (Phil. 4:19). Believers today should faithfully support those ministries and missionaries that are faithfully and obediently endeavoring to preach the Gospel, teach God's Word and contend for the faith in this needy, sin-cursed world.

3. In 2 Corinthians 9:12, the apostle Paul specifically tells the church at Corinth that financial giving supplies the

needs of the saints. He adds that such giving is also a great cause for thanksgiving by those who benefit from the ministry of God's Word.

D. Giving is an act of worship to God.

  1. Philippians 4:18 reveals that we worship God through our giving. God accepted the Philippian believers' gifts to the ministry as a "sacrifice" that was acceptable and well-pleasing to Him. To give a sacrifice or offering to God is an act of worship.

  2. Hebrews 13:15-16 reminds us that we must not forget to "do good and to communicate ... for with such sacrifices God is well pleased." To *communicate* in this text, means to give of our resources. We must share with others and give back financially to our Lord. To do so is to worship and obey our Savior.

E. Giving proves our love for God.

  1. Second Corinthians 8:7-8 reveals that we can back up our professions, or "prove [our] sincerity" and love for God, by giving.

  2. In Matthew 6:19-21, Jesus tells us that how we handle material wealth is a gauge that measures our spiritual health.

II. The Amount to Give

A. According to ability

  1. The New Testament Scriptures do not dictate a universal percentage or dollar amount to be given back to God. Rather, the believer is simply commanded to give, and he is reminded of what God has given Him and

that everything he possesses belongs to God and is merely entrusted to him. This reality should stir the faithful believer to give as much as possible back to God for the work of the ministry.

2. We are commanded, as a starting point, to give according to that which we are able to give. The Word of God tells the believer to give "as God hath prospered him" (1 Cor. 16:2) and says everyone should give "as he purposeth in his heart" (2 Cor. 9:7).

B. Give beyond ability (sacrificially) at times

1. While all believers can give back to God, sometimes God blesses us with extra money to give, or other times He lays it upon our hearts to give more to His work, even though it might mean we will need to sacrifice some of our own wants.

2. The apostle Paul praised God for the believers in Macedonia because they freely gave beyond their means, even though they were extremely poor and experienced great suffering and persecution (2 Cor. 8:1-5). Ideally, believers should, like the Macedonians, give generously to the work of the Lord with all liberality (2 Cor. 9:5, 11, 13).

III. Our Attitude Toward Giving

Our understanding, or lack thereof, concerning the importance of giving will determine whether or not we possess the right attitude about giving. Obviously, if we fully realize the price that Jesus Christ paid for our sins and are mindful of the sacrificial gift given to us by the Father, then we will not think twice when we are called upon to give something back to our Savior. On the other hand, if we do not understand or appreciate the importance of Christ's gift, or if we neglect to be continually mindful of it, then to give anything back to our Lord becomes an unpleasant necessity to us.

The Word of God, by precept and example, encourages us to give willingly and cheerfully to the work of the Lord. Giving is one way in which we bear fruit in our Christian lives, and such fruit will be rewarded one day (Phil. 4:17).

A. Willingly

1. In 2 Corinthians 8:12, Paul says the believer must have a "willing mind" concerning the matter of giving. Likewise, in 2 Corinthians 9:7, we are commanded to give "not grudgingly, or of necessity." Rather, we are to give out of the willingness of our hearts.

2. The grace of giving should be accomplished not only in a spirit of willingness but even in a spirit of eagerness (2 Cor. 9:2). Paul actually "boasted" to other Christians about the "forwardness" or "eagerness" of the Corinthian believers' attitude toward giving. They were ready to give and looking forward to providing for the needs of the Lord's work.

B. Cheerfully

1. Not only should we give willingly, but we should also give in a spirit of cheerfulness. Paul wrote that we should give cheerfully, "for God loveth a cheerful giver" (2 Cor. 9:7).

2. Clearly, if our offerings to God are to be "an odour of a sweet smell, a sacrifice acceptable, wellpleasing to God" (Phil. 4:18), then they must be given in a spirit and attitude of joy, gladness and cheerfulness. It is impossible to please God with our gifts and offerings if our hearts are far removed from our actions.

One renowned pastor and Bible teacher of the past, A. C. Gaebelein, wrote concerning the believers' willingness to give: "God Himself delights to give. In infinite love He gave His only begotten Son, and He delights in all who imitate Him in His ways. There is no compulsion in giving save the constraint of His love." The love of our Savior should motivate us to give gifts and offerings back to Him. We will be blessed if we give willingly, cheerfully and abundantly, for God reminds us that we will one day obtain reward in heaven for giving accordingly (Matt. 6:19-20). Such future reward only further reveals the grace and love of our Savior who bestows upon us so much more than we ever deserve.

Study Questions

1. What should serve as the motivation for our giving to the Lord?

2. In addition to monetary giving, what are some other ways that believers can give to the Lord's work?

3. According to 2 Corinthians 9:7, who is commanded to give?

4. What are some of the purposes for giving to the Lord's work?

5. According to 1 Corinthians 16:2 and 2 Corinthians 9:7, is there a specific amount that believers are commanded to give? Explain.

6. According to Philippians 4:17, how does the believer benefit from giving?

7. According to the following verses, how is the believer to give to the Lord?

    *   2 Corinthians 8:12

    *   2 Corinthians 9:2

    *   2 Corinthians 9:7

15

Money and
Material Possessions

Both the Old and New Testament Scriptures are full of information detailing the believers' proper relationship to money and material possessions. God certainly does not want us to be ignorant concerning these matters. In a day when so many men, women and children are caught up in the desire for wealth and entrenched in a culture of materialism, the child of God must firmly grasp some basic Biblical principles concerning his possessions and apply these principles to his life if he is to honor and glorify God.

I. Understand That Everything That Exists Belongs to God

Psalm 24:1 reminds us that "The earth is the LORD's, and the fulness thereof; the world, and they that dwell therein." We must remember that God created the heavens and the earth and everything therein (Gen. 1:1; Col. 1:16), and as the Creator of all things, He is the Possessor of all things.

II. Understand That Everything You Possess Is a Gift From God

A. Not only has our Savior created all things and not only has He given us the gift of eternal life through His death, burial and resurrection, but He has also met all our physical, material needs as well. As the Creator of heaven and earth, it is He who has bestowed all blessings and mercies upon us. James writes, "Every good gift and every perfect gift is from above, and cometh down from the Father of lights" (James 1:17). John the Baptist told his disciples, "A man can receive nothing, except it be given him from heaven" (Jn. 3:27). Paul reminded Timothy that it is God "who giveth us richly all things to enjoy" (1 Tim. 6:17).

B. Since God is the Creator and true Owner of all things, we must realize that everything we "own" is actually God's to do with as He pleases. We are simply stewards, that is, managers of that which He has entrusted to us. This reality should motivate us to utilize that which we possess in an efficient, responsible manner.

III. Be Content With What God Has Given You

A. Some individuals have been blessed with more money or material possessions than others. But regardless of the depth of our pocketbooks, we must realize that God has given us that which He desires for us to possess, and His will is always best. Therefore, we must be content with what God has entrusted to us (Heb. 13:5).

B. Specifically referring to money, Paul told the Philippian believers that he had learned to be content with that which God had provided for him, for he realized that it was not money or material possessions that endued him with strength and motivation for ministry (Phil. 4:11). On the contrary, he says, "I can do all things through Christ which strengtheneth me" (Phil. 4:13). He understood that Christ alone was his strength and motivation for ministry.

C. Paul told Timothy that "godliness with contentment is great gain" (1 Tim. 6:6). Why? "For we brought nothing into this world, and it is certain we can carry nothing out. And having food and raiment let us be therewith content"

(1 Tim. 6:7-8). Because this earth and all our material possessions are only temporary, we should be content, or satisfied, with fulfilling God's will and gaining reward that is eternal (1 Cor. 9:25).

IV. Realize That You Cannot Serve God and Wealth Simultaneously

A. The Word of God teaches us that it is impossible to serve both God and money. In Matthew 6:24, Jesus said, "No man can serve two masters: for either he will hate the one, and love the other; or else he will hold to the one, and despise the other. Ye cannot serve God and mammon (wealth or money)." To *serve* in this context means "to give priority to." Earlier in the text, Jesus commanded His disciples to lay up treasure in heaven rather than on earth (Matt. 6:19-20). We must give priority to the acquisition of spiritual treasure rather than money and material possessions, which are corruptible and often turn us away from fidelity toward God.

B. To make the acquisition of money and material possessions our priority in life reveals that our heart is not devoted to our Savior. Jesus said, "For where your treasure is, there will your heart be also" (Matt. 6:21). Those who are living to serve themselves are not serving God. Those who are living to serve God are not serving their own fleshly desires. Devotion to the world and devotion to God are mutually exclusive (Jas. 4:4; 1 Jn. 2:15).

V. Be Aware That Money Can Ensnare You

A. God's Word repeatedly warns about the dangers of money (1 Tim. 6:6-11). The following references from Proverbs are especially noteworthy with regard to the accumulation of wealth: Proverbs 11:4, 28; 13:7; 18:10-12; 23:4 and 28:20, 22. While money is not inherently evil, the believer is often tempted to serve money and change his priorities in life as a result of money, thus foregoing a proper relationship with God. Remember, we cannot serve God and mammon at the same time.

B. Paul tells us that "they that will be rich fall into temptation and a snare, and into many foolish and hurtful lusts, which drown men in destruction and perdition," adding that "the love of money is the root of all evil" and noting that those who are serving money have "erred from the faith, and pierced themselves through with many sorrows" (1 Tim. 6:9-10).

C. Although many feel as though money is a means of safety and security, they are deceived, for money actually provides a false sense of security and serves to enslave those who place their faith and trust in it. What should be the Christian's response to the enticing lure of money and material possessions at the expense of Godliness and truth? "But thou, O man of God, flee these things" (1 Tim. 6:11).

True spiritual riches can be obtained by those who are financially poor, while those who possesses great physical riches can potentially dwell in spiritual poverty (Prov. 13:7). Clearly, the believer should seek to lay up treasure and riches in heaven rather than upon the earth. Those believers who have been blessed with wealth and material possessions must be sure to focus their attention and priority upon God while responsibly managing that which God has entrusted to them (1 Tim. 6:17-19). Those who have not been blessed with great wealth should be content with that which God has given to them and refrain from covetousness, as it will only lead to spiritual ruin.

Study Questions

1. According to Psalm 24:1, who rightfully owns everything that exists?

2. According to the following verses, who has given us everything we possess?

   • John 3:27

   • 1 Timothy 6:17

   • James 1:17

3. What should our attitude be concerning the things we possess and the things we do not possess, as revealed in the following verses?

   • Philippians 4:11

   • 1 Timothy 6:6-8

   • Hebrews 13:5

4. According to Matthew 6:19-20, what should be our primary investment while on the earth?

5. What are some ways in which we can lay up treasure in heaven?

6. What important principles did Jesus state in Matthew 6:19 and 24?

7. What was Paul's advice to Timothy in 1 Timothy 6:11 should he ever be tempted to pursue the riches of this world rather than the riches in Christ?

8. Read Proverbs 13:11. What is the Scriptural way by which we can gain the money necessary to meet our needs?

16

Dealing With Sin in Our Life

Because we all are born with a sin nature, we are separated from fellowship with God and possess a propensity to sin. Every aspect of our being—our mind, emotion, intellect and will—is affected by this sinful nature. We cannot please God on our own, no matter how hard we try. We are sinners by our very nature as well as by the deeds of sin we commit. Yet when we believe in Jesus Christ, trusting Him alone for our salvation, we become a "new creature" and receive a new nature (2 Cor. 5:17).

As children of God, we now have the ability to walk in fellowship with Him and honor and glorify Him through obedience to His Word. However, our old nature is still present within, and we will sometimes yield ourselves to this sinful nature and obey it rather than yielding to the indwelling Holy Spirit. But as Christians, we now have the power to break free from the reigning power of sin as a result of our new nature. The Word of God tells us how we can have the power over sin in our life when we do fall short of God's will. The Bible is our Guidebook for living, revealing not only all that we need to know concerning life and Godly living but also how to overcome any sin that has crept into our lives.

I.   Understand That Sin Affects the Life of the Believer

A. Sin hinders a proper relationship with God — While we can never lose our salvation, we can lose our close fellowship with God by allowing sin to come between us and our Lord. In Psalm 66:18, David writes, "If I regard iniquity in my heart, the Lord will not hear me." The apostle John adds, "If we say that we have fellowship with [God], and walk in darkness, we lie, and do not the truth: But if we walk in the light, as He is in the light, we have fellowship one with another, and the blood of Jesus Christ His Son cleanseth us from all sin" (1 Jn. 1:6-7). Just as an offence can hinder a close relationship between a son and a father or a mother and a daughter, sin can cause fellowship with our Heavenly Father to be broken. Yet He is still our Father. Our status as His children can never be broken.

B. Sin will cause a loss of reward at the Judgment Seat of Christ — The Bible tells us that as believers, we all will one day appear before the Judgment Seat of Christ, and we will receive reward (or lose reward) according to our works, whether they are good or bad (2 Cor. 5:10). To sin now will cause loss of reward later.

C. Sin brings God's chastisement — Not only will we lose future reward as a result of sin, but we will eventually be disciplined by our Heavenly Father while on earth. Notice Hebrews 12:5-11. God chastens us so we will not continue to live in sin. Love is the underlying motive for His chastisement.

II. Acknowledge Your Sin Before God

A. The act of confession — When we realize that sin affects our lives in such a negative manner, we will certainly desire to repent and return to a right relationship with God. In order to do so, we must "confess our sins," that is, we must see our sins as God sees them. First John 1:9 provides the guidelines for a renewed relationship with God. We must agree that our sins are evil and reprehensible in His sight and that they hinder our relationship with Him. When we do confess any known sin in our lives, we know that God "is faithful and just to forgive us our sins, and to cleanse us from all unrighteousness."

B. The benefits of confession — Jesus Christ taught His disciples to ask for forgiveness of sin in their lives (Lk. 11:4), and as believers today, we too should follow Christ's directive if we desire to maintain fellowship with Him. We are to confess any known sin to God. As a result of this confession, we will realize three benefits according to 1 John 1:9.

   1. God "is faithful and just to forgive us our sins" that we have recognized and confessed to Him. We can know for sure that if we confess our sin to Him, He will not only hear us but He will restore us to a right relationship with Him.

   2. God will "cleanse us from *all* unrighteousness." As believers, our lives are riddled with "secret faults"— sins we have committed that we do not even realize. David understood the importance of cleansing from all sin when he prayed, "Search me, O God, and know my heart: try me, and know my thoughts: And see if there be any wicked way in me..." (Psa. 139:23-24). Likewise, David prayed, "Cleanse Thou me from secret faults" (Psa. 19:12). When we confess our known sin, our hearts become right with God, and He promises to cleanse us not only from our confessed sin but from *all* unrighteousness.

   3. This complete cleansing allows for the third benefit, namely, renewed fellowship with God. We can be sure that He now hears and answers our prayers since we

are walking according to His will (Psa. 66:18; 1 Jn. 5:14-15).

III. Follow God's Guidebook for Righteous Christian Living

A. Through the regular study of God's Word, we can know how to maintain a proper relationship with God and, therefore, resist our old nature's tendency to continue in sin. In Psalm 119:11, David writes, "Thy Word have I hid in mine heart, that I might not sin against Thee." In order to hide God's Word in our hearts and refrain from sinning, we must study His Word regularly.

B. God's Word is completely sufficient to teach us how to overcome sin in our life. Second Timothy 3:16-17 tells us that the Bible is profitable for doctrine, for reproof, for correction and for instruction in righteousness so that we can become mature believers who are equipped to do works that are pleasing to our Lord. It is through the milk and meat of the Word of God that we can grow spiritually into the kind of believers God desires us to be (1 Pet. 2:1-2).

C. When the desire to sin arises, we can use God's Word as an offensive weapon against our evil desires. Ephesians 6:17 tells us we should take "the sword of the Spirit, which is the Word of God" and use it to battle against the forces of evil. This sword of the Spirit, combined with the rest of the Christian armor described in Ephesians 6:11-17, will enable us to have victory over sin.

Study Questions

1. Using 1 Corinthians 6:9-11 and Ephesians 2:2-6, contrast the old nature and the new nature.

2. According to the following verses, what happens when a believer allows sin to remain in his life?

    *   Psalm 66:18

    *   1 Corinthians 3:12-15

    *   Galatians 6:7-8

    *   2 Timothy 2:16

    *   Hebrews 12:5-11

    *   1 John 1:6

3. How can we rid our lives of sin and return to proper fellowship with the Lord according to 1 John 1:9?

4. What are the benefits of confession according to 1 John 1:9?

5. According to the following verses, how should we handle those sins we unknowingly commit?

   • Psalm 19:12

   • Psalm 139:23-24

6. Once we have dealt with the sin in our lives, what steps should we then take to maintain our renewed fellowship with God according to the following verses?

   • Psalm 119:11

   • Ephesians 6:11-17

   • 2 Timothy 2:15

   • 2 Timothy 3:16-17

   • 1 Peter 2:1-2

17

The Rapture of the Church

The return of Jesus Christ for His church is our "blessed hope," that is, our glorious expectation (Titus 2:13). As members of His body, we will one day either die, should our Lord tarry, or we will be caught up in the air to meet Him, should He return while we are still alive (1 Thess. 4:16-17). This return of Christ for the church is called the "rapture." Although our English Bible never specifically uses the word *rapture*, the Scriptures clearly foretell the reality of such an event. The word *rapture* is derived from the Latin translation of the Greek word for "caught up" as stated in 1 Thessalonians 4:17.

It is important for us to remember that the rapture (when Jesus Christ returns *for* His church) and the second coming of Christ (when Jesus Christ returns to earth *with* His church to rule and reign on the earth in His millennial kingdom) are two separate events that will occur at two separate times. Because the rapture of the church is the next event to occur on God's prophetic timetable, this lesson will specifically focus on this glorious event.

I. The Time of the Rapture

A. The rapture is imminent

1. *Imminence* does not mean that an event must happen right away; rather, it means that an even can happen at any time. Jesus Christ could return for His church at any moment. No other prophetic events need to occur before Jesus Christ can return to catch us away to Himself.

2. The writers of the New Testament believed that Jesus Christ could return for the church at any moment. They firmly believed that the rapture was imminent. Notice the following authors' statements and, specifically, the presence of personal pronouns ("we," "us"), as they relate to the writers' belief that they, too, would be a part of the rapture of the church:

   a. Paul — 1 Thessalonians 1:10; 5:6; Titus 2:13; 1 Corinthians 15:51-52
   b. John — 1 John 2:28
   c. James — James 5:7-8
   d. Peter — 1 Peter 4:13; 2 Peter 3:10-15
   e. Jude — Jude 21, 24

3. The writers of the New Testament taught the imminent return of Christ. For example, Paul exhorted Titus to "look" for Christ's return (Titus 2:13), and he urged the Thessalonian believers to "watch" and "wait" for the return of Christ (1 Thess. 1:10; 5:6). Likewise, the apostle John encouraged the readers of his epistle to be ready for Jesus' return so they would not be ashamed before Him at His coming (1 Jn. 2:28).

B. The rapture occurs prior to the tribulation period

   1. Some pastors and Bible teachers erroneously teach that Christ will return to catch away the church either during the midst of the seven-year tribulation period or following this time of great trouble and calamity that

shall come upon the whole world. On the contrary, the Word of God teaches that Christ will return for His church prior to the seven-year tribulation period.

2. The Bible teaches that believers will be saved "from" or "out of" (Gr: *ek*) the coming wrath that God will pour out upon the whole world (1 Thess. 1:10; Rev. 3:10). As soon as the "Restrainer" is removed from the earth, the tribulation period will begin (2 Thess. 2:3, 7). The Holy Spirit is the one who restrains the culmination of evil, and it is He who indwells believers. When the believers are removed from the earth, the Holy Spirit is also removed, and the Antichrist will be free to begin his great works of iniquity. At that point, the seven-year tribulation begins (2 Thess. 2:1-12).

II. The Nature of the Rapture

A. Christ will return in the air — At the rapture, Jesus Christ will return in the air and will not set foot upon the earth. The apostle Paul describes Christ's return as follows: "For the Lord Himself shall descend from heaven with a shout, with the voice of the archangel, and with the trump of God … then we which are alive and remain shall be caught up … to meet the Lord in the air." (1 Thess. 4:16-17).

B. The bodies of Church-Age believers who have died will be resurrected — The souls of all Church-Age believers who have already died will return with Christ at the rapture, and their dead bodies will be resurrected (1 Thess. 4:14-16). At that time, they will receive new, glorified bodies (1 Cor. 15:50-52).

C. Living believers will be caught up to meet Christ in the air — At the rapture, all living Christians will be "caught up together with them (the resurrected believers) in the clouds, to meet the Lord in the air" (1 Thess. 4:17). At that time, we, too, will receive our glorified bodies (1 Cor. 15:50-53).

III. Our Response to the Rapture

A. We need to be ready

1. We live today in light of what we believe will happen in the future. If we truly believe that Jesus Christ could return at any moment, then we will do everything we can to be ready for His return. The imminent return of Christ should motivate us to live Godly lives, to witness to the lost and to encourage and edify fellow believers.

2. After describing the reality of the rapture and our victory over death, the apostle Paul then states, "Therefore, my beloved brethren, be ye steadfast, unmoveable, always abounding in the work of the Lord, forasmuch as ye know that your labour is not in vain in the Lord" (1 Cor. 15:58). The reality of Christ's imminent return should motivate us to remain steadfast in the faith and abound in His work.

3. The apostle John tells us to "abide" (remain in close fellowship) in Christ. Why? "That, when He shall appear, we may have confidence, and not be ashamed before Him at His coming" (1 Jn. 2:28). Clearly, Christ's imminent return should motivate us to always be in close fellowship with Him.

B. We need to evangelize

1. If we truly believe Christ could return for us at any moment, then we will take every opportunity to tell others about the Good News of Christ's substitutionary death and resurrection before it is too late. Remember, after the rapture, God will pour out His wrath upon

the whole world.

2. Jesus told His disciples He was preparing a place for them in heaven and He would return and take them to that place (Jn. 14:1-4). Thomas then asked, "Lord, we know not whither Thou goest; and how can we know the way?" Jesus responded, "I am the way, the truth, and the life: no man cometh unto the Father, but by Me" (Jn. 14:6). The only way any individual can participate in the glorious return of Christ for His saints is to believe in Jesus Christ, for He is the way, the truth and the life. We must proclaim this glorious truth to all.

Study Questions

1. What promise does Jesus make in John 14:1-3?

2. Could Jesus Christ return for us at any moment? Explain from Scripture what the apostles believed concerning the imminent (any moment) return of Christ.

3. What words does Titus 2:13 use to describe the rapture of the church?

4. When Christ returns for His church, who will be caught up to be with Him first according to 1 Thessalonians 4:16?

5. Who will be caught up to be with Christ next according to 1 Thessalonians 4:17?

6. Will the rapture occur before or after the seven-year Tribulation period? Explain using Scripture.

7. What kind of bodies will we receive at the rapture according to 1 Corinthians 15:50-53?

8. How should the fact of Christ's imminent return impact the life of the believer?

18

The Judgment Seat of Christ

The doctrine of the Judgment Seat of Christ is perhaps one of the most neglected or misunderstood doctrines in the church today. Yet this doctrine is vitally important to know and understand, for our future reward, or lack thereof, is determined by the way that we live our lives right now. The reality of the future Judgment Seat of Christ should motivate us to live a life that is well-pleasing to our Lord and Savior, Jesus Christ, for He will one day evaluate our earthly works.

While our "works" certainly do not earn us any merit or favor in God's eyes with respect to our salvation, we are responsible *as Christians* to do those works that glorify God and are pleasing in His sight. As we walk in the Spirit, we produce the fruit of the Spirit and grow thereby. At the Judgment Seat of Christ, our salvation is not in question. Rather, the works we have accomplished (or failed to accomplish) while on this earth and the motives behind our works will be evaluated and judged by Jesus Christ. The Word of God reveals the participants, the purpose and the place and time of this future event.

I. The Participants in the Judgment Seat of Christ

A. Second Corinthians 5:10 says "we" must appear before

Christ at the Judgment Seat. Likewise, in Romans 14:10, Paul writes that "we shall all stand before the Judgment Seat of Christ." In these verses, Paul is writing to Church-Age saints. This includes every Christian since the beginning of the church on the day of Pentecost until the rapture of the church when Christ returns in the air to catch us away to be with Him.

B. The apostle Paul exhorted Timothy to labor fervently for the Lord since Christ will judge both the living and the dead at His return (2 Tim. 4:1-2, 8). Timothy, like us, lived during the Church Age and will, like us, be judged at the Judgment Seat of Christ.

C. The apostle John wrote that we (Church-Age believers) are to monitor our actions and conduct in order to be certain that we do not lose reward (2 Jn. 8). It is clearly evident that all Church-Age saints (including all believers who are studying this lesson) will one day stand before Christ at the Judgment Seat.

II. The Time and Place of the Judgment Seat of Christ

A. The time

1. The Judgment Seat of Christ will occur following the rapture of the church. Paul told the Corinthian believers that they were forbidden from judging the motives of other believers because Jesus Christ would "bring to light the hidden things of darkness, and will make manifest the counsels of the hearts" when He returns for the church (1 Cor. 4:5).

2. Paul also told Timothy that the Lord will reward faithful believers "at that day" (2 Tim. 4:8). We see from the context of this verse that "that day" refers to the time when Jesus Christ will return and judge those believ-

ers who are both alive and dead (2 Tim. 4:1). Therefore, the rapture will occur (dead and living believers
will ascend to be with Christ) and then the Judgment
Seat will convene.

3. Jesus Christ tells us that we need to be ready for His
    coming, for at that time He will distribute rewards and
    "give every man according as His work shall be" (Rev.
    22:12). The Judgment Seat of Christ will occur imme-
    diately after the return of Jesus Christ.

B. The place

1. Because the Judgment Seat of Christ occurs immedi-
    ately following the rapture of the church, this event
    will convene in heaven. In John 14:1-3, Jesus Christ told
    His disciples that He would return and take them up
    to His Father's house which He was preparing for them
    in heaven. At the rapture, Christ will return for us and
    take us up to heaven to His Father's house. At that
    time, the Judgment Seat of Christ will take place.

2. Prior to his discussion concerning the Judgment Seat
    of Christ, Paul told the Corinthian believers that to be
    absent from the body is to be present with the Lord (2
    Cor. 5:8). When we are "present with the Lord" in
    heaven, we will be judged according to our works,
    whether they had been good or bad.

III. The Purpose of the Judgment Seat of Christ

A. The purpose of the Judgment Seat of Christ is to deter-
    mine the believer's rewards according to his works while
    on earth. According to 2 Corinthians 5:10, Jesus Christ will
    judge our earthly deeds to determine whether or not they
    are worthy of reward. Paul told the Corinthian believers,
    "Every man's work shall be made manifest" (1 Cor. 3:13).

B. All Church-Age believers will either receive reward or loss of reward according to their works (2 Cor. 5:10) as well as the motives behind their works (1 Cor. 4:5). Paul describes all our works as "good or bad."

1. Good works are any deeds accomplished according to the will of God that are classified as "rewardable" in the eyes of the Lord. Our works will be rewarded on the basis of:

   a. Their quality (1 Cor. 3:13)
   b. The attitude and manner in which they were accomplished (1 Cor. 4:2)
   c. The motive for which they were accomplished (1 Cor. 4:5)

2. "Bad" works are those deeds that are not accomplished according to the will of God and that God does not deem to be rewardable. *Bad* in this context means "good for nothing" or "worthless" in the eyes of God.

C. It is important to understand that the purpose of the Judgment Seat of Christ is not to determine one's eternal destiny, for those who will stand before Christ at this judgment are already believers and will spend eternity with Jesus Christ. Neither is the purpose of the Judgment Seat of Christ to punish believers for their sins, for all our sins have already been forgiven by Christ at the very moment we believed in Him. All our sins — past, present and future — have already been forgiven and covered by the shed blood of Jesus Christ (Col. 2:13).

As believers, we must fulfill the will of God for our lives and strive to obtain a "full reward" at the Judgment Seat of Christ (2 John 8). If our works and motives are not deemed "rewardable" by our Savior, then we will suffer loss of reward (1 Cor. 3:13). While God's Word does not expressly state the extent to which our rewards (or lack thereof) affect our future status or service for Him, it does seem as though our rewards relate to the extent to which we will rule and reign with Christ during the Millennium and throughout all eternity (1 Cor. 6:2-3; Rev. 4:4; 5:10; 20:4). Certainly such a reality should motivate us to live Godly lives and to be "blameless" at the appearing of Jesus Christ (1 John 2:28).

Study Questions

1. According to 2 Corinthians 5:10 and Romans 14:10, who will be judged at the Judgment Seat of Christ?

2. When will the Judgment Seat of Christ take place according to 1 Corinthians 4:5 and 2 Timothy 4:1-8?

3. Where will the Judgment Seat of Christ take place (Jn. 14:1-3)?

4. According to the following verses, what are some things we can do to inherit future reward?

   • Proverbs 11:18

   • 1 Corinthians 3:14

   • 1 Corinthians 9:16-17

   • 2 Timothy 4:8

- James 1:12

5. According to the following verses, will believers receive punishment or reward at the Judgment Seat of Christ?

   - Matthew 16:27

   - 1 Corinthians 3:14-15

   - 1 Corinthians 4:5

   - 2 John 8

6. How do we know that the Judgment Seat of Christ is not for the purpose of determining one's eternal destiny?

7. How should our knowledge of the Judgment Seat of Christ affect our lives today?

To order additional copies of *Biblical Basics for Believers,* complete the information below (please call for special discounted bulk quantity rates):

Ship To: (please print clearly)

Name: _____

Address: _____

City, State, Zip: _____

Phone: _____

_____ copies of *Biblical Basics for Believers* @ $10.00 each $ _____

Postage and handling @ $2.00 per book $ _____

CA residents add 7.25% sales tax $ _____

Total amount enclosed $ _____

Make checks or money orders payable to:

Fundamental Evangelistic Association
P. O. Box 6278
Los Osos, CA 93412

— —

To order additional copies of *Biblical Basics for Believers,* complete the information below (please call for special discounted bulk quantity rates):

Ship To: (please print clearly)

Name: _____

Address: _____

City, State, Zip: _____

Phone: _____

_____ copies of *Biblical Basics for Believers* @ $10.00 each $ _____

Postage and handling @ $2.00 per book $ _____

CA residents add 7.25% sales tax $ _____

Total amount enclosed $ _____

Make checks or money orders payable to:

Fundamental Evangelistic Association
P. O. Box 6278
Los Osos, CA 93412

Other publications available from the Fundamental Evangelistic Association:

Foundation Magazine

Foundation: A Magazine of Biblical Fundamentalism is a bi-monthly publication that seeks to provide the Bible-believing Christian with information he can use to "earnestly contend for the faith" in the days in which we live. *Foundation* contains credible information concerning the developments, programs and strategies of the movements against which the faithful believer must contend; instructional and devotional articles and Bible studies written by Fundamentalists of past and present for the purpose of teaching the Word, preaching the Gospel and contending for the faith; firsthand reports of major religious meetings from an admittedly Fundamentalist perspective and current religious news items and commentary designed to keep the believer up-to-date. A free sample copy is available upon request.

Feature: A Daily Bible Study Guide

Feature is a daily Bible study guide written by Fundamentalists for Fundamentalists. *Feature* seeks to direct the reader into a diligent study of the truths of God's Word each day rather than simply providing a "thought for the day." It uses only the King James Version and is published on a quarterly basis. Special bulk prices are also available for those individuals or churches who need three or more copies per quarter. A free sample copy is available upon request.